# DINGHY COACHI

GW00734004

This handbook is for all those working, or coaching staff within the National Sailing ( Schemes. It replaces previous editions o Although the basic principles of teaching ~~........~ ..~.~ ..~. ~..~..~~~, ..... ~~....~.. contains alterations in certain areas reflecting the revision of the RYA National Dinghy and Keelboat Schemes in 1998. This book will remain valid until the next revision in 2003.

Text:              James Stevens and John Driscoll

Cover photo:   RYA
Illustrations:   Phil Twining


The RYA is grateful to the following people

*Maureen Crouch* and *David Truan* of the NSPCC for their help and advice on the section on protecting children from abuse

*Debbie Brown* of Sailability for her section on sailing for the disabled

*Simon Davies* for the section on teaching single handed sailing

*Mike Hart* for the section on Advanced Instructor training

*The National School Sailing Association* for giving us permission to re-produce some of the games used in their book 'Sailing Across the Curriculum'

*Phil Twining* for the section on Senior Instructor training

*Caroline Stevens* for reading and correcting the proofs

Published by

**The Royal Yachting Association**

RYA House  Romsey Road  Eastleigh  Hampshire SO50 9YA

©1999 Royal Yachting Association

# CONTENTS

# INTRODUCTION

The National Sailing Scheme is taught in a vast number of locations from the open sea to small lakes, from the north of Scotland to the shores of the Mediterranean. The boats vary from Optimists and Picos to keelboats and include the new generation of high performance asymmetric spinnaker dinghies. In spite of this variation, the process of learning to sail has remained largely unchanged during the thirty years that the RYA has run a national training scheme.

The 'RYA method' known to every dinghy instructor has stood the test of time and with a few modifications remains as effective today as it was at its inception. This book explains the method along with all the other skills and knowledge required by RYA instructors. It assumes you are already a competent sailor who would like to become involved in an RYA recognised school, teaching dinghy or keelboat sailing.

The two booklets G14 and G7 have been combined into this one publication. An explanation of who can teach the scheme and where is included, along with a space to include your log of instructional experience.

James Stevens

RYA National Coach

# REQUIREMENTS FOR RYA RECOGNISED TEACHING ESTABLISHMENTS

Only recognised establishments can issue RYA certificates. These establishments fall into three main categories:

**Sailing centres open to the public;**

**Sailing clubs which provide tuition for their members and prospective members;**

**Organisations such as local education authorities, Scouts and HM Services who are restricted to teaching their own groups or members.**

RYA recognition is vested in the Principal and implies that certificated courses are run and that the remainder are closely associated with the aims of the National Sailing Scheme. The Principal is responsible for issuing RYA certificates and ensuring that the requirements of RYA recognition are maintained at all times.

An initial application fee is payable by all new recognised establishments. Thereafter, an annual subscription is payable to the RYA, except in the case of establishments who are already subscribing as affiliated clubs or associations.

Full details of the recognition procedure and requirements are available from the RYA along with a Principal's Pack containing more in depth information for new and prospective Principals. Briefly, the criteria for dinghy and keelboat sailing centres are as follows:

Each centre will be inspected annually to ascertain that:

1 The Principal or Chief Instructor holds a valid RYA Senior or Keelboat Instructor certificate, as appropriate;
2 The instructors hold the appropriate valid RYA instructor certificates;
3 The student:instructor ratios do not exceed those laid down in the syllabus for each level of course, ie;

| Type of craft: | Student:instructor ratio: |
|---|---|
| Crewed dinghies | 3:1 |
| Single handed dinghies | 6:1 (applies only whilst the boats are used as single-handers) |
| Keelboats | Keelboats with accommodation 5:1 (Instructor on board) |
| | Dayboats/keelboats without accommodation Maximum 4 students per boat. 1 instructor must be responsible for no more than 9 students (eg 3 boats with 3 students in each boat) |

4 The establishment's teaching syllabus meets the requirements of RYA certificate courses;
5 The onshore teaching facilities are adequate for the proposed operation;
6 Boats provided for tuition are suitable, seaworthy and in good repair;
7 Safety boats satisfy all the requirements for the operating area and are properly equipped to carry out the combined duties of teaching platform and rescue boat;
8 All students and instructors will be in possession of personal buoyancy appropriate to the sailing area and type of boat in which they are receiving instruction, and will be required to wear this equipment on occasions when prevailing conditions make its use necessary;
9 The Principal understands the requirements of the RYA as to the proper running of a recognised teaching establishment;
10 The Principal understands his responsibilities for training his staff in teaching techniques, powerboat handling and house rules relating to health and safety issues;
11 All activities will be covered by adequate public liability insurance (at least £1,000,000);
12 RYA logbooks will be available to all students and RYA certificates will be issued to all those who successfully complete the course.

**Recognition of Overseas Establishments**

Sailing schools permanently based outside the United Kingdom must meet the following criteria:

1 The establishment is owned and operated by a British based organisation;
2 The primary language of instruction is English;
3 The establishment shall have a permanent address abroad and a contact address in the UK;
4 The establishment shall pay the overseas recognition fee and the costs of annual inspection visits, including transport, accommodation and subsistence.

All other requirements for UK establishments also apply.

# *WITHDRAWAL OF RECOGNITION*

The RYA Training Committee can withdraw recognition for contravention of the rules or spirit of recognition.

A school wishing to appeal against withdrawal of recognition may bring their case to an RYA tribunal which will be convened for the purpose.

## How to apply for RYA Recognition

Please refer to the Guidance Notes for full details of the requirements for recognition. If you wish to make an application, follow the procedure shown below:

Principal or Chief Instructor holds appropriate RYA qualifications

▼

Complete the Application for Recognition and send it to RYA HQ with the fee. Also send your credit account application form if you wish to open an account for buying publications.

▼

The RYA will send a copy of your application for recognition to your Regional Coach or Liaison Officer who will nominate an Inspector and contact you to arrange a date for inspection.

▼

Complete the shaded sections of the Centre Inspection Report form and keep it ready for your Inspector to complete the rest.

▼

Your Inspector will need to see some training in action. This training could be, for example, an introductory session for some volunteers or in-house training for staff. The Inspector will be looking for good standards of tuition, safety and supervision.

▼

Upon satisfactory completion of an inspection, the report will be sent to RYA HQ with a recommendation to grant recognition which will be confirmed to the Principal.

If you need further advice on applying for recognition, contact either the Training Division at RYA HQ, or your Regional Coach/Liaison Officer. When you have been allocated an Inspector, they will also be able to offer advice prior to their visit.

## Advertising

Recognised schools may use the RYA logo, details of which are available from the RYA. Schools must ensure that they do not use the name of the RYA to advertise any activities not covered by the terms of recognition.

## Swimmers

It is strongly recommended that all those participating in the sport of sailing should be able to swim. No minimum level swimming ability is stipulated, but students should be able to demonstrate water confidence. It is essential that the instructor in charge of a course knows if any course members are non-swimmers. Non-swimmers may be required to wear life jackets instead of buoyancy aids.

## Duty of Care

Instructors must always remember that they are usually teaching relatively inexperienced sailors, who may not be able to make a sound assessment of the risks inherent in the sport. Instructors should not hesitate to make prudent decisions in unfavourable conditions.

## *Health Declaration*

All RYA recognised teaching establishments are strongly advised to include a health declaration in their booking forms. Such information must be passed on by the Principal to the individual instructor responsible for the student.

One possible format is given below:

Details of any medical treatment being received (if none, write 'none'):

_____

_____

_____

I declare that to the best of my knowledge, I am not suffering from epilepsy, disability, giddy spells, asthma, angina, or other heart condition, and I am fit to participate in the course.

Signature                                              Date

The information sent out to students should stress that illnesses or medical conditions need not necessarily prevent them from taking a full part in the course, but the Principal or instructor must be aware of any potential problems. If a student is in any doubt about fitness to take part in a course, his GP should be able to advise.

# WHO TEACHES WHAT

**PROFICIENCY COURSES**

| | Young Sailors Scheme | National Sailing Scheme (dinghies) | National Sailing Scheme (keelboats) |
|---|---|---|---|
| Dinghy Instructor | Start Sailing 1, 2 & 3 Advanced Red & White | Levels 1, 2 & 3 | |
| Keelboat Instructor | | | Levels 1, 2 & 3 |
| Club Racing | Racing Red & White | Level 4 | Level 4 (if also keelboat instructor) |
| Advanced Instructor | Advanced Blue | Level 5 | Level 5 (if also keelboat Instructor) |
| Racing Coach | Racing Blue | | |

**INSTRUCTOR TRAINING**

| Course | Taught by | Moderated by | Ratio |
|---|---|---|---|
| Assistant Instructor | Senior Instructor | N/a | |
| Dinghy Instructor | Coach/Assessor | Coach/Assessor | 1:6 plus Moderator |
| Keelboat Instructor | Coach/Assessor authorised by RYA HQ | Coach/Assessor authorised by RYA HQ | 1:6 plus Moderator |
| Tidal Endorsement | Coach/Assessor | N/a | 1:6 |
| Advanced Endorsement | Coach/Assessor | N/a | 1:6 |
| Keelboat Endorsement | Coach/Assessor authorised by RYA HQ | N/a | 1:6 |
| Multihull Endorsement | Coach/Assessor | N/a | 1:6 |
| Club Racing Coach/Racing Instructor | Racing Coach | N/a | |
| Senior Instructor | Coach/Assessor | Coach/Assessor (throughout the course) | 2:8 |
| Racing Coach | National Racing Coach | N/a | |
| Coach/Assessor | National Coach | | |

# I WANT TO BE AN RYA INSTRUCTOR

**16** — *Minimum age*

**Level 2** — *National Powerboat Certificate*

**First Aid** — *Certificate*

**Level 5** — *Sailing ability equivalent*

**Pre-entry** — *Sailing assessment*

**Do course** — *Attend five day instructor training course run by RYA Coach/Assessor, with continuous assessment and moderation by another Coach.*

## *I ALSO WANT TO GET AN NVQ*

The process of obtaining an NVQ for dinghy instruction can be started at any time during or after the process above. Further details can be found on page 106

# REQUIREMENTS FOR
# RYA COACHING AWARDS

## THE ASSISTANT INSTRUCTOR AWARD

This award provides recognition of the local training given to experienced sailors intending to qualify as RYA Dinghy or Keelboat Instructors.

### Role

The Assistant Instructor is a competent small boat sailor, who has been trained to assist Instructors with teaching sailing up to the standard of the National Sailing Certificate Level 2 and the Start Sailing Stages 1, 2 and 3 of the Young Sailors Scheme. They must work under the supervision of an RYA Senior Instructor (for dinghy sailing establishments) or the Chief Instructor of a keelboat teaching establishment.

### Eligibility

Candidates must hold the National Sailing Certificate Level 3 or Young Sailors Advanced White Badge.

### Training

Training and assessment are conducted by the Principal or Chief Instructor of an RYA recognised teaching establishment who holds a valid RYA Senior Instructor certificate (for dinghy sailing establishments). The training may be based on a 20 hour course covering the RYA teaching methods for beginners outlined on page 39.

### Assessment

Candidates will be assessed on their practical teaching ability with beginners. Successful candidates will have their Log signed and will be awarded an RYA Assistant Instructor certificate by their Principal.

### Certificate Validity

The Assistant Instructor Certificate awarded to successful candidates is valid only at that establishment for five years and will not normally be renewable.

### Important Note

As the training and assessment is limited to the role of assisting qualified instructors and does not include first aid or powerboat handling, Assistant Instructors must never be allowed to work without direct supervision.

It is normal practice for every Principal to ensure that all his staff are conversant with the teaching techniques and local 'house rules' of that establishment. Thus if an Assistant Instructor moves from one recognised teaching establishment to another, it is likely that his new Principal will issue a new Assistant Instructor Award after retraining.

# DINGHY/KEELBOAT INSTRUCTOR

In 1998, the dinghy and keelboat training schemes were amalgamated to form the National Sailing Scheme. It is possible to complete the scheme in either dinghies or keelboats. Instructors teaching the scheme must be qualified for the type of boat in which they will be teaching, ie only RYA Dinghy Instructors can teach in dinghies, and only RYA Keelboat Instructors can teach in keelboats. The instructor certificate is endorsed accordingly and will also show whether the instructor is qualified to teach on inland or tidal waters (depending on where they completed the course).

## Role

The Instructor is a competent and experienced small boat sailor, capable of sailing a training boat confidently in strong winds and handling small powerboats. The Instructor has been assessed as competent to teach dinghy or keelboat sailing to adults and children, both beginners and improvers, up to the RYA National Sailing Certificate Level 3 or Young Sailors Advanced White badge.

Although responsible for teaching individuals and small groups, the Instructor has not been assessed as competent in running a sailing school, and should always work under the supervision of an RYA Senior Instructor (for dinghy courses) or the Chief Instructor of a keelboat teaching establishment.

## Eligibility

Candidates must fulfil the following criteria before taking part in the instructor training course:

Minimum age 16 (no candidates will be accepted for training under this age)

Valid first aid certificate: either the RYA's First Aid Course, or one recognised by the Health and Safety Executive, covering the treatment of hypothermia and a minimum of six hours course length.

RYA Powerboat Level 2 certificate.

Pre-entry sailing assessment completed within one year prior to the instructor training course (details given on page 35).

## Training

Training in teaching techniques afloat and ashore is provided during the instructor training course, which is staffed by RYA Coach/Assessors. The course will be based on a five-day week of 50 hours, but may take the form of a number of weekends, single days or sessions at the discretion of the organiser. Courses run on a protracted basis like this may take slightly longer than the 50 hours to allow for revision time. Candidates should apply to RYA HQ or their Regional Coach for a list of instructor courses.

## *The course will include:*
a) The structure of the National Scheme
b) Training in RYA teaching methods to Level 3 including teaching those with special needs
c) Instructing techniques for adults and children
d) Preparation and presentation of a lesson
e) Preparation and use of visual aids
f) The assessment of students' abilities
g) The revision of all subjects covered up to Level 3
h) A one-hour written paper (or oral test) covering teaching methods and background knowledge
i) The use of powered craft in a teaching environment

Throughout the course, evidence of competence in these areas will be noted by the training Coach/Assessor and credited towards the candidate's final assessment.

## *Assessment*
The assessment will usually take place on the final day of the training course and will be carried out by a Coach/Assessor who has not been involved in or associated with the training of the candidates. Candidates will be required to demonstrate competence in the following areas:

Course preparation
Course delivery
Course management
Customer liaison

The assessment will take place in a conventional teaching environment, preferably using real beginners as students.

## *Certificate Validity*
Instructor certificates are valid for five years from the date of issue, provided that a valid first aid certificate is maintained. Every five years, the certificate must be sent to the Regional Coach for revalidation, along with a log of instruction experience since qualifying, a valid first aid certificate and the appropriate fee or RYA membership number. Before revalidating the certificate, the Regional Coach will check the log for evidence of recent instructing at an RYA recognised establishment. If little or no experience is shown, it may be necessary for the instructor to attend a reassessment in order to ensure that he is up to date with current practice.

## *Note*
It is possible for instructors to complete their training course in multihulls and have their certificates endorsed to show that they are Multihull Instructors. However, the more common route to obtaining this qualification is to first qualify as a Dinghy Instructor and then complete a two-day Multihull endorsement course. Please see the following section on Instructor Endorsements.

# INSTRUCTOR ENDORSEMENTS

Whilst an RYA Instructor can teach students up to Level 3 of the National Sailing Scheme, it should be the aim of every instructor to gain endorsements to the basic qualification. The following endorsements are designed to extend the scope of an instructor's ability and will increase his value to the Principal of a recognised teaching establishment.

## TIDAL ENDORSEMENT

### Role

This endorsement should be obtained by instructors who completed their initial training course and assessment inland, but who subsequently want to instruct at a coastal establishment.

### Training

Candidates should apply to their Regional Coach for details of courses. Training will be given by an RYA Coach/Assessor. Candidates will be required to attend a two-day course during which they should demonstrate the pre-entry sailing test skills and teaching techniques in tidal waters.

### Assessment

Candidates will be assessed on a continuous basis afloat by the training Coach/Assessor. Upon successful completion of the course, their logbooks will be signed by that Coach/Assessor.

## ADVANCED INSTRUCTOR ENDORSEMENT

### Role

The Advanced Instructor is an experienced instructor with a wide background of sailing experience who has been trained to teach sailing to the standard of the RYA National Sailing Certificate, Level 5.

### Eligibility

Candidates will hold the RYA Instructor certificate and will have recorded at least one season's experience of teaching sailing since obtaining that certificate. Candidates will be skilled to the level of the requirements of the National Sailing Certificate, Level 5 and should have previous powerboat handling experience in a teaching environment.

### Training

Candidates should apply to their Regional Coach for details of courses. Candidates will be required to attend a two-day course covering the teaching of boat handling, seamanship skills and navigation to the required standard.

### Assessment

Candidates will be assessed on a continuous basis afloat, and by a written theory test. Upon successful completion of the course, their logbooks will be signed by their Coach/Assessor.

### Note

Candidates who are trained and assessed inland are qualified to teach Level 5 courses inland only and will be required to attend a further coastal conversion before being qualified to teach Level 5 courses at coastal venues.

## KEELBOAT INSTRUCTOR ENDORSEMENT

### Role

This endorsement should be obtained by instructors who completed their initial training course and assessment in dinghies, but who subsequently want to instruct in small keelboats.

### Training

Candidates should apply to their Regional Coach for details of courses. Training will be given by an RYA Coach/Assessor with relevant keelboat experience, and who has been authorised by the RYA to run Keelboat Instructor training. Candidates will be required to attend a two-day course during which they should demonstrate the pre-entry test skills and teaching techniques.

### Assessment

Candidates will be assessed on a continuous basis afloat. Upon successful completion of the course, their logbooks will be signed by the course organiser.

## MULTIHULL INSTRUCTOR ENDORSEMENT

### Role

This endorsement should be obtained by instructors who completed their initial training course and assessment in dinghies, but who subsequently want to instruct in multihulls.

### Training

Candidates should apply to their Regional Coach for details of courses. Training will be given by an RYA Coach/Assessor with relevant multihull experience. Candidates will be required to attend a two-day course during which they should demonstrate the pre-entry test skills and teaching techniques.

### Assessment

Candidates will be assessed on a continuous basis afloat. Upon successful completion of the course, their logbooks will be signed by their Coach/Assessor.

# CLUB RACING COACH/RACING INSTRUCTOR

## Role

The Club Racing Coach is an experienced racing sailor who has been trained to teach racing skills at Red and White Badge level in the RYA Young Sailors Scheme, to run RYA Level 4 and Introductory Racing courses at clubs/teaching establishments, and to assist RYA Racing Coaches.

The Racing Instructor is a Club Racing Coach who is also qualified as an RYA Dinghy or Keelboat Instructor.

## Eligibility

Candidates should have at least five years' experience of dinghy racing, including at least one open, area or national championship.

Valid first aid certificate: either the RYA's First Aid Course, or one recognised by the Health and Safety Executive, covering the treatment of hypothermia and a minimum of six hours course length.

## Training

Training will take the form of a two-day course covering the preparation, practice and management of running basic racing courses. The course has a high practical content and it may be necessary for candidates to provide a boat.

Candidates should contact their Regional Race Training Co-ordinator for details of courses, which are organised on both a multi-regional and a regional basis. Each course will have a minimum number of candidates.

## Course Content

The course will include:

a) The Structure of the National Race Training Scheme
b) Organisation, preparation and management of Level 4, Introductory, Red and White Badge courses
c) Instructional technique afloat including the use of race training exercises
d) Working from coaching boats
e) The preparation and presentation of a racing topic
f) Use of visual aids, including YR8, the RYA OHP Resource Pack.

## Resources available from the RYA

Introductory race training video "Capture the Wind"
RYA Book of Race Training
G14 Dinghy Coaching Handbook
G11 Young Sailors Logbook
YR8 Overhead Projector Resource Pack

## Assessment

Candidates will be assessed on a continuous basis, afloat and ashore. Effective communication skills in addition to the appropriate level of racing knowledge are important factors in the assessment.

The areas of assessment include:

a)  Knowledge of the sport
b)  Sailing and racing ability
c)  Communication skills afloat and ashore
d)  Organisational ability afloat and ashore.
e)  Presentation

Upon successful completion of the course, the Club Racing Coach Assessor or Regional Race Training Co-Ordinator will sign the candidate's logbook. If the candidate provides evidence of a valid First Aid certificate, the RYA Award is effective immediately.

## Certificate Validity

RYA Club Racing Coaches and Racing Instructors are required to complete a one-day reassessment every three years. This will be co-ordinated on an annual basis by an authorised RYA Regional Race Training Co-ordinator.

## Further Training

Coaching skills can be developed by assisting an RYA Racing Coach. Club Racing Coaches with suitable experience (usually two seasons' minimum) may be recommended for training as RYA Racing Coaches by a Class Association, Regional Race Training Co-ordinator or National Racing Coach.

Some clubs and teaching establishments may require evidence of competence in powerboat handling. The most commonly accepted form of evidence for basic handling is the National Powerboat Certificate Level 2, but this does not cover the rescue boat skills included in the Safety Boat Course

Club Racing Coaches are encouraged to attend National Coaching Foundation Key Courses in order to improve their coaching techniques.

# RYA SENIOR INSTRUCTOR

## Role

The Senior Instructor is an experienced instructor who has been assessed as competent to organise and manage sailing courses within the RYA National Sailing Scheme.

The Senior Instructor is qualified to organise and control group sailing tuition and to supervise and assist instructors. Such a person must be a confident, competent manager, capable of organising groups of all ages and directing the work of his instructors.

An RYA recognised dinghy/keelboat teaching establishment must have a current Senior Instructor as its' Principal or Chief Sailing Instructor.

## Eligibility

Candidates must first be an RYA Dinghy Instructor and must fulfil the following criteria before taking part in the Senior Instructor training course:

Minimum age 18

Two years intermittent or one year full time dinghy instructing since qualifying

RYA Safety Boat certificate or Level 4 certificate (pre-1996)

Valid first aid certificate: either the RYA's First Aid Course, or one recognised by the Health and Safety Executive, covering the treatment of hypothermia and a minimum of six hours course length.

Signed recommendation from the Principal of an RYA recognised establishment (see page 120).

Sailing ability to at least the standard of RYA Dinghy Instructor (an assessment may be necessary if sailing ability cannot be adequately demonstrated during the training course)

## Training

Candidates should apply to their Regional Coach for details of courses, which are run on a regional basis with a minimum of six candidates. Courses are organised by the Regional Coach and staffed by two or more RYA Coach/Assessors. The course will be based on a five-day week of 40 hours, but may take the form of two long weekends or three weekends at the discretion of the organiser.

## Assessment

The assessment will be continuous and will be made by at least two Coach/Assessors. Candidates will be required to demonstrate competence in the following areas:

Personal sailing ability
Course preparation
Course delivery
Course management
Customer liaison

## Certificate Validity

Senior Instructor certificates are valid for five years from the date of issue, provided that a valid first aid certificate is maintained. Every five years, the certificate must be sent to the Regional Coach for revalidation, along with a log of instructional experience since qualifying, a valid first aid certificate and the appropriate fee or RYA membership number. Before revalidating the certificate, the Regional Coach will check the log for evidence of recent instructing experience at an RYA recognised establishment. If little or no experience is shown, it may be necessary for the instructor to attend a reassessment in order to ensure that he is up to date with current practice.

# RACING COACH

## Role

The Racing Coach is a highly experienced, accomplished racing sailor capable of running class association racing clinics and Blue Badge racing courses within the RYA Young Sailors Scheme. Specialist coaches may be appointed to cover individual subjects such as meteorology, fitness or mental training.

## Eligibility

Candidates should have competed with distinction at regional, national or international regattas and be fully conversant with technical aspects of racing. Some prior experience in training or teaching is essential. Candidates should apply in writing, and their application should be endorsed by a Class Association or Regional Race Training Co-ordinator. This does not guarantee acceptance for training.

Candidates must hold a Club Racing Coach or Racing Instructor qualification and have attended two National Coaching Foundation courses.

## Award

To achieve the award, candidates should complete the following, preferably in the order given:

- Valid first aid certificate: either the RYA's First Aid Course, or one recognised by the Health and Safety Executive, covering the treatment of hypothermia and a minimum of six hours course length.
- Evidence of competence in powerboat handling may be required by some clubs and teaching establishments. The most commonly accepted form of evidence for basic boat handling is the National Powerboat Certificate Level 2 but this does not cover the rescue boat skills included in the Safety Boat Course.
- Coaching experience: Assist an RYA National Coach or an experienced Racing Coach with class association race training or a Blue Badge course for at least two weekends.
- National Coaching Foundation Key Course: Complete a Key Course in one of the following subjects:
    Delivering the goods - coaching methods and communication
    Coaching children - coaching children and young people
    Mental preparation for performance - motivation and mental toughness
- Training Course: Satisfactorily complete a two-day course run by RYA HQ. The course will include:
    The structure of the National Race Training Scheme
    Course planning, resources and management
    The coaching of boat handling, boat speed and tactics
    Preparation and presentation of theoretical subjects
    An introduction to sports psychology
    Fitness, diet and injury prevention

### Resources

Introductory race training video 'Capture the Wind'
YR8 Overhead Projector Resource Pack
RYA Book of Race Training

### Certificate Validity

The award must be completed within two years of attending the training course, or the course should be repeated. All coaches should attend a one-day revalidation not less than each second year. This requirement also applies to candidates in the process of completing the award.

# COACH/ASSESSOR

The Coach/Assessor is an experienced Senior Instructor who has been assessed as competent to train and assess Instructors and Senior Instructors.

### Eligibility

- Senior Instructor with proven ability, ie a high level of personal sailing ability, good teacher and motivator, good fleet manager and leader, enthusiastic.
- Recommendation from Regional Coach.

### Training

Consists of three parts:
- Preparation/selection weekend
- Five-day training course
- Apprenticeship

#### Preparation/selection weekend

Candidates should be able to:
- Demonstrate any part of the National Sailing Scheme syllabus levels 1 to 5
- Sail competently in a variety of dinghies including singlehanders and high performance craft
- Plan and manage a course involving sessions ashore and afloat
- Handle a rescue boat
- Give a classroom presentation including the use of visual aids
- Show enthusiasm, motivation and leadership

#### Training course

The training course will include:
- The skills of teaching and assessing RYA Dinghy Instructors including the Advanced and Multihull endorsements.
- The RYA National Sailing Scheme and standards required for instructional awards including the administration of the scheme.
- Advanced seamanship techniques
- High performance dinghy sailing
- Techniques of Senior Instructor training
- Teaching students with special needs

**Apprenticeship**

Candidates who complete the course successfully will be invited to work with an experienced Coach/Assessor until a recommendation is made by their Regional Coach that they should be appointed.

Coaches wishing to teach Keelboat Instructors must attend a separate course organised by the RYA.

Coaches wishing to become Inspectors of teaching establishments must attend a one-day training course organised by the RYA.

## *Coach Updating*

The appointment is for five years, following which Coaches must attend a short practical updating course organised by the RYA. The update will include:

- Techniques for teaching and assessing instructors
- Information on changes to the scheme
- An opportunity to feedback to the RYA
- A personal sailing test

# INSTRUCTIONAL TECHNIQUES

Sailing instruction is essentially a process of brief - task - debrief. The students are there to handle the equipment and actually do the tasks.

The learning really starts afloat and in particular when the student takes the helm. The instructor's job is to make this experience enjoyable, informative and safe.

On a course you should start sailing as soon as possible. A safety brief, correct clothes and a demonstration are essential but don't spend time talking about the theory of sailing at this stage. Students are usually slightly anxious about their first sail and stories about dangers and disasters will do little to allay their fears. Once people see the boat and equipment being used, or better still, are using it themselves they will pick up the concept fairly quickly. Also, the sooner you can give a student a straightforward achievable task followed by a genuine 'well done', the sooner they will relax and realise the course is achievable.

## *Briefing*

You must be able to explain clearly what is required. This is virtually impossible across the water from a moving powerboat or to a frightened student in a heeling dinghy. Brief ashore or, if afloat, calm down the situation by lying to or heaving to.

A demonstration is an excellent way of showing the task required. The National Sailing Scheme incorporates a progression of demonstrations, some of them ashore (the land drills), which allow students to observe and then handle the controls without any distractions.

When giving a demonstration make sure everyone can see and then draw their attention to the part of the boat that is important at the time. This might be the tiller, the luff of the jib, or possibly the sideways effect of the tide.

*You cannot instruct clearly across the water or from a moving powerboat.*

Make your briefings exactly that - brief. The anecdotes can come later, and remember the purpose of the demonstration is to teach a new skill not to display your prowess. Your brief has failed if the students are unclear about what they are supposed to be doing. Good instructors can deliver and summarise the brief as a succession of related 'bullet points' which are clear and easy to remember. A few questions at the end will help to reinforce the points made.

*...casionally allow a mistake to be made.*

## *The Task*

The task must be chosen to suit the ability of the student. Part of the skill of instructing is to assess the student's ability and provide tuition at a challenging but not impossible level. It is very frustrating for someone with a natural flair or with some experience to be taught at the pace of the slowest beginner.

Once the task has been set, allow the student to feel responsible for it. Do not continually interrupt - if you have briefed well it should be unnecessary. If events start to go wrong a quiet word will allow the student to correct the mistake while still being in control. Never elbow students out of the way to demonstrate your skill, the idea is that they demonstrate theirs.

Occasionally, if you can, allow a mistake to be made to illustrate a point, but only do this if you feel it is a good learning opportunity. It is a technique more appropriate to the higher level courses and you should take great care not to use the situation to put down or demoralise the student.

*A notebook can be a bit threatening.*

## Debriefing

Debriefing is one of the most important skills of the sailing instructor. Done well it is informative, positive, good-natured and helpful. Done badly it can be destructive and demoralising.

At the end of a debrief the students should be clear about what happened, their strengths and weaknesses and be fired with enthusiasm to try again. They should never lose their self esteem or motivation.

Debrief as soon as possible after the task. If you are in the boat with the students, heave to. If you are teaching single handers, stop regularly.

You must observe each task very carefully both to give feedback to individuals as well as the group. A notebook is helpful if you are in a rescue boat or ashore but can be a bit 'official' and threatening in a dinghy.

A good way of debriefing is to ask the student what happened or if they would act differently next time. Your comments should reinforce what was done well but you must also be clear about what needs improvement. The instructor's personality comes in here. It is important to be able to deliver advice on how to correct mistakes without any 'edge' or bad feeling. Students want to know what they did wrong but do not want to be 'ticked off' or feel their instructor is using the occasion to deliver a personal slight.

*Students do not want to be 'ticked off'*

The standard form of debrief starts with a recognition of what went well followed by the errors made and finishes with encouragement on how to improve. A few questions will give the student an opportunity to give their point of view and ensure that the instructor knows that the point has been received. Many instructors used to taking charge and issuing commands neglect the students comments and are therefore unaware as to whether they are learning anything.

## *Keeping students informed*

RYA certificates provide a great incentive to book on courses. Unfortunately because a measure of competence is involved they can become a discouragement to the weak student who feels a failure as the prospect of a certificate fades, particularly at the higher levels of the scheme. Your Chief Instructor will advise on the importance of keeping everyone informed as to their progress through the course, explaining where they are now and what they can realistically achieve. This could involve breaking the news that a level 5 certificate might not be possible by the end of the week. Temper this by explaining what can be achieved and agree between you to get the best possible value out of the course. From then on you are acting as a coach, setting goals and pointing out strengths and weaknesses and offering encouragement. Point out how much has been achieved as the week progresses so that by the final debrief you can both be satisfied that the course was worthwhile.

If you fail to keep students informed, tension will build up with students discussing amongst themselves whether they are passing or failing, and during the final debrief your teaching may be blamed for lack of results. This lack of communication between instructor and student is one of the most common reasons for complaints about RYA courses. Remember that many of the people you teach are highly successful and respected in their own field. The only skill you may have that they haven't is the ability to sail and teach sailing. You must ensure they retain their dignity and a positive attitude towards you and the sport. Do not underestimate this part of the job - it is one of the most skilful aspects of instructing. Really talented instructors receive letters of thanks from students who have not been awarded a certificate.

## *Your first course*

Experienced, confident instructors were all anxious about teaching their first course. Your best plan is to arrive early and get to know the area and boats. Your Chief Instructor will ensure you know the 'house rules' and where the equipment is stowed. Make a list of the points you wish to make during the teaching session.

When the students arrive, welcome them and ask them about themselves and their experience. Learn their names immediately. Explain what you are going to do and invite them to ask about anything they do not understand. If you come across as sincere, the students will be willing you to succeed, even if your teaching technique is unpolished. Be honest about your experience.

Avoid giving them an over-inflated view of yourself or you will lose their confidence.

If you make an error admit it, think clearly and put it right. No-one gives perfect demonstrations every time but you should be able to stay in control and correct a misjudgment.

Being slightly nervous before your first course is a good quality - it shows you care and want to make it a success. At the end, thinking of the things you should have done during the course is also a good quality - it means you are evaluating and improving what you do.

The Principal of the school is there to give you help and advice. Use it.

## *Ten Instructor Qualities*

**1. Competent sailor**
Not necessarily brilliant, but capable, competent and reassuring

**2. Good communicator**
Articulate and clear, good listener, doesn't continually talk about themselves

**3. Good teacher**
Can explain clearly using visual aids where necessary, can structure a lesson

**4. Coach**
Can assess progress and provide individual goals and tuition

**5. Honest and straightforward personality**
Can deliver criticism and praise without personal prejudice.  No 'edge'

**6. Conscientious**
Takes care over delivery of course and the boats and equipment

**7. Sensitive**
Adjusts delivery to suit individuals and takes interest in students

**8. Enthusiastic**
Own enjoyment of the sport is infectious even in adverse conditions such as no wind

**9. Responsibility**
Understands responsibility for safety of students, stays in charge even when things go wrong

**10. Knowledgeable**
 Understands the subject and RYA scheme

# PREPARING AND PRESENTING LESSONS ASHORE

## *TEACHING ASHORE*

With small groups, much of the teaching is done informally around the boat or a portable board. With larger groups it is necessary to use some classroom teaching techniques. A lecture is not always the most effective way of teaching a practical subject like sailing. For example a bowline can only be taught by giving the students a rope and helping them to tie the knot. Merely stating a fact is no guarantee that your students will have received the information.

**Bear the following points in mind when teaching:**

- Before the first session welcome the students onto the course.
- An informal start helps you to find out who they are and their experience. It is less daunting if you have met everybody before standing in front of them.
- Learn the students' names as soon as possible.
- Find out their experience: this will help you pitch the course at the right level.
- Consider the room layout.
  Anything you say or do will be pointless unless your students can see and hear you. Encourage your students to fill classrooms from the front. Make sure your room is comfortable, cool and well ventilated.
- Keep talks short.
  Twenty minutes is about the right length of time to maintain students' attention without testing or a break. Don't over-run.
- Outline your aims at the beginning of a lesson and summarise the essential points to remember at the close.
- A handout stating the important facts is useful, but should not be given out until the end of the lecture. Handouts distributed at the beginning will only be read by students when they should be listening to you.

- Give your talk a structure: Introduction, Development, Summary, Test.
- Draw on practical examples to illustrate your points.
  Anecdotes should not be used to reinforce your personal brilliance - the class will quickly sense they are being taught by a knowledgeable and credible sailor without you having to remind them regularly.
- Consider the age and experience of your audience (see notes on teaching adults).
- Technical language.
  Avoid complicated terms but define any which are essential. Before you answer questions on, say, sailing by the lee, ensure

*This may be too relaxed for some talks*

that the rest of the class know what you are talking about.

- Choose your position.
  Where and how you stand will have an effect on your talk. Standing behind a desk or lectern may appear more formal and puts a barrier between you and your audience. Sitting on a table at the front of the class may be too relaxed for some talks. Watch polished speakers and assess their use of body language. Don't hide behind your visual aids (see page 28).
- Involve your students.
  Speak to all of them. Don't talk to the ceiling, the floor or the wall at the back of the classroom. Try to make eye contact with every member of the audience at some stage. As alternatives to a monologue, use question and answer techniques, discussions etc and use students' names.
- Avoid irritating mannerisms.
  Your RYA instructor course will help to identify habits of which you may have no knowledge.
- Avoid distractions.
  Like mannerisms, any distractions which take your students' attention away from what you are saying will damage your talk. If you are giving a talk outside because of good weather, arrange the group so that they are facing away from any distractions and such that the sun is in your eyes, not theirs.
- Practise writing on blackboards and/or whiteboards.
  Prepared overhead projector acetates are preferable to copious board-writing with your back to your students. Never talk to your board, always to your students. If you are not using or have finished with a board, rub it clean to avoid distraction.
- Don't bluff.
  If you don't know the answer to a question - say so. Your students would far rather have an honest 'don't know, but I'll find out' than a bluffed answer. Having said that, you should always ensure that you have a wider knowledge of your subject than the basic facts contained in your lecture.
- Don't be afraid to test.
  Providing the questions are not threatening they can be used to maintain interest and will help to reinforce your teaching.
- Avoid sarcasm, humiliation or rudeness.
  Try not to let any of your prejudices alienate members of the class. In particular, avoid patronising students of a very different age group from your own and avoid sexism.
- Don't try to be funny unless you are naturally witty.
  The instructor course will help to appraise you of your natural level of humour.

*Avoid patronising students*

Finally, remember that your talk will have succeeded only if all your students leave it having learnt all the important facts which you intended to communicate and are eager to learn more.

## *Teaching adults...*

- Adults tend to have a greater fear of failure than children.
  They are therefore more reluctant to appear foolish in front of a class. You should concentrate on rewarding ideas and not on making those who give wrong answers feel inadequate. Adults will accept being corrected if it is done positively and is not humiliating.
- Adults for whom 'being lectured' is their only experience of being taught are initially reluctant to become involved in discussion, question and answer, tests and quizzes etc. Encourage them to ask questions and take part in the discussion. You will have to push against this dislike at first; once the students have overcome it they will learn more quickly and enjoy themselves more. Don't give anyone the opportunity to opt out. To encourage others, congratulate those who do join in initially.
- Adults are much more vulnerable to sarcasm than children, who tend to be used to it.
- The greater part of adult learning since leaving school will have been by 'problem-solving' and personal experience. Use this to your advantage and let 'problem-solving' from information you supply be one of your teaching methods, but remember that this approach usually takes longer than instructions.
- An adult's academic interest in the subject is not always compatible with his practical ability; the gap sometimes widens with age.

## *...and children*

- Generally, young people usually make better students than adults, learning faster and with better retention.
- However, they are intolerant of poor classroom teaching. If their motivation is not high, it will be lowered further by a dull lecture in the classroom. Children learning within a group of relative strangers may initially be very shy about contributing answers. This in turn makes it difficult for the instructors to assess how much is being absorbed without resorting to testing, which again makes the process seem like school. Once you have overcome the shyness, however, you could find the opposite problem of having to control class input to the level which allows you to teach.
- Teaching young children (6-10) to sail requires a different approach to that used for older children or adults. The subject is covered well in the International Optimist Club Guide .
- Remember to explore the alternatives to the lecture: games ashore, work-cards, modelling or drawing sessions.

# PREPARATION AND USE OF VISUAL AIDS

Sight accounts for about 75% of input, hearing about 15% and other senses share the remaining 10%.

**Basic principles**

- Relevance

  Visual aids should not be produced for their own sake. They must be relevant or they become a distraction.

- Clarity

  Diagrams must be easily understood and not contain irrelevant detail. They must be readable by the furthest of your audience. Any visual aid which cannot be seen by everyone is neither visual nor an aid.

- Timing

  Don't produce visual aids until they are needed; they will only distract your audience if displayed too soon. Dispose of them after use.

- Display

  Try to display a visual aid in a dramatic manner. Students will remember something for longer if it is linked to a highlight.

- Involvement

  A display of neatly tied knots on a board is much less effective than students attempting to tie the knots themselves, although the knotboard will be useful for reference after the lesson.

- Use the other senses

  An aid which can be passed around is more valuable than something which is merely displayed. Beware of moving on to another topic while your visual aid is still circulating. Nobody will listen to you if they have a toy with which to play. Equally, use the mechanism of some visual aids to 'punctuate' your lecture and put in 'paragraphs' ie, switching off the OHP between acetates, lights on/off between slides.

- Yourself

  Don't forget that you are a walking visual aid with optional sound yourself. Think about your mannerisms, delivery, position etc and their effect on the class. Never hide behind another visual aid such that your audience cannot see you properly. Finally, dress for the occasion. Although sailing is a practical sport, don't let your appearance serve as a distraction to your audience. A good general rule is to dress as well as the best dressed of your audience - that way, nobody will be offended.

## Types of visual aid

It is often said that the best visual aid available to the sailing instructor is the boat itself, but the more advanced your teaching, the less true that statement becomes. Each of the other visual aids in common use has certain advantages and drawbacks.

- Chalkboard or penboard

  These are widely available and can be portable. Be careful to talk to your students and not to the board. The disadvantages are that although adequate for simple messages or drawings it is unsatisfactory for detailed work to be done when the audience is present.

- Flipchart

  This has many of the characteristics of the chalkboard but the twin advantages that it is portable and information can be stored and used repeatedly.

- Overhead projector

  Properly used, this is undoubtedly the most versatile visual aid employed in sailing centres. Although it requires power, it can be used in daylight and without the instructor losing eye contact with the audience.

  Although it is possible to write and draw as you speak, most instructors prefer to prepare OHP slides in advance. You can enhance them by the use of colour and by using overlays to build up or break down complex concepts or techniques.

  Once a few operating tricks are learnt, the OHP is simple to use effectively but you must avoid the temptation to put too many words on an acetate. Remember that words are not visuals, even though they may be used to trigger thoughts or retain ideas.

  If you have a choice, position the screen in the corner of the room so that you are less likely to obstruct anyone's view.

- 35mm transparencies

  Commonly used for subjects like capsize recovery, spinnaker handling and advanced boat handling techniques, 'home-made' transparencies have the added advantage that the boats and background will be familiar to the students.

  Be ruthless when editing your transparencies into a final teaching sequence.

- Video

  Either use professionally produced videos or a video camera afloat with your group.  The RYA's videos are intended to be used in sections with the instructor interspersing the video with practical sessions. If using a video camera afloat consider the following:

  Forget about the attractions of the zoom lens. Get as close to the action with as short a focal length as you can. The resulting picture will be far steadier and hence less likely to induce seasickness in the audience later.

  Turn off the microphone. Even the professionals separate the roles of cameraman and commentator. Your 'off-the-cuff' comments are more likely to offend and be less helpful than a later commentary over a silent video.

  Choose definite techniques or manoeuvres to film and switch off in between. Nothing is more aggravating for your students than having to sit through two hours of playback for the two minutes of their own sailing.

- Models

  Ranging from simple shapes used for collision avoidance talks to detailed models of sailing dinghies, the scope for models is limited only by the ability of the builder.  In general, a model should have only enough detail as is required to ensure a full understanding of its role.  Over-complication may be satisfying to the creator but must not detract from its use as a visual aid.

## AVOIDING COMPLAINTS

Most complaints arise from a lack of communication.

A common problem occurs when a student who has attended and passed the basic Level 2 course, wishes to take a Level 3 or 5 course with virtually no further experience and without the ability to achieve the standard by the end of the week. Ideally the person taking the booking will have spotted this

*How dare you criticise MY centre!*

and either diverted the student to a more suitable training course or ensured that their aims are realistic. If not, the instructor has the job of redefining what can be achieved during the week. Someone who has paid for a Level 5 course is expecting to receive the syllabus as defined in the logbook. If this level is inappropriate the instructor should discuss realistic aims and ensure that the student agrees. A degree of tact and diplomacy is required to break this news but most people who have struggled on the first day will welcome a relief from the stress of trying to achieve an unrealistic target. Leave the possibility of the certificate open as people often improve once the pressure is off.

If you do not inform people of their progress you are more likely to receive a complaint along the lines of 'I didn't achieve the certificate because I wasn't taught well'.

One of the pleasures of instructing is meeting a variety of different people but occasionally one turns up who, for whatever reason, is likely to complain. If you can spot one of these, try to run the course exactly by the logbook, this handbook and your school's operating procedure. Before the end of the course while there is still sailing time available ask if they are satisfied with the course and if they would like to practise any further skills or techniques. Before the end of each sailing session try to elicit some feedback and give opportunities for comment. The Principal or Chief Instructor should also give opportunities for feedback as the course progresses. We cannot expect every course to be perfect, equipment fails and the weather is unpredictable but providing you have delivered the course to the best of your ability and to the guidelines of your school and the RYA, the students on the receiving end should realise that the course was worthwhile.

If a school receives a complaint the Principal or Chief Instructor should deal with it personally. Try to establish what the complainant is asking for. An immediate and understandable reaction is 'how dare you criticise my centre' but a more helpful attitude is 'how can we resolve this?' Often the simplest option is to offer more tuition. If you can arrange this, perhaps at a later date, before they leave your centre you can save a lot of correspondence and bad feeling.

The instructors who receive the fewest complaints are those who are competent, take an interest in their students, and ensure that even the difficult or weak students feel they are an important part of the group. The instructional skills required are well beyond those of just sailing or even just teaching.

# TEACHING DISABLED SAILORS

Teaching a disabled person to sail is exactly like teaching a non disabled person. You mix common sense with experience and apply safe practice.

The overall objective is to learn how to sail effectively, develop confidence, enjoyment, a sense of achievement and to have fun. It is important to encourage maximum participation and activity by people. Do not prejudge a person's competence by their disability, but rather by their experience, knowledge and ability.

We are all individuals each with different interests. Someone with a disability has ideas, makes plans, gets excited, even bloody minded - in short they are just like the rest of us. There is no need to adopt a different manner and vocabulary or to feel sympathy or embarrassment. The important thing is to treat a disabled person as you would anyone else.

**Communication is the key to success.**

It is essential to ensure that communication is a two way process, it is about talking and listening.

Key points to remember are:
- Never assume
- Ask
- Listen
- Establish individual communication
- Emphasise the ability not disability
- Make the terminology/jargon understandable
- Build trust
- Check understanding
- Offer empathy not sympathy
- Learn very basic sign language

A disability is not a barrier to the successful completion of courses. All participants must be able to demonstrate their ability to complete the whole syllabus, but this can be achieved by proxy. A candidate who cannot perform a task directly must be able to satisfactorily direct a third party to achieve that task on their behalf. It is worth bearing in mind that the candidate has to possess good communication and teaching skills as well as knowing how to undertake the manoeuvre.

The 'special endorsements' line of the certificate should be treated with care. Do not list any disability unless it affects the holder's aptitude directly in the handling of a boat. The prosthesis that gives a user complete function is of no consequence. However, a visually impaired person may have the endorsement 'Requires visual assistance on the water'.

Sailability will answer any questions or give advice and can offer local and national Awareness Training. For further information contact 01703 627449.

# THE ASSESSMENT OF YOUR STUDENTS' ABILITIES

## Young Sailors Scheme

The syllabi for each of the stages of the start Sailing and Advanced Sailing Awards are clearly expressed in terms of competencies. As the student is able to do each item, so it can be signed off. When all the items for a particular award are complete, the certificate or sticker may be given. On any course, it is possible that some students will complete some extra items from the next stages, in which case those items can also be signed off.

## Level 1 - Start Sailing

The aim of the Adults Level 1 course is to get people afloat in a relaxed, enjoyable manner. The emphasis is on practical teaching techniques. To gain the Level 1 certificate, the student simply has to demonstrate each of those techniques whilst being taught.

## Level 2 - Basic Skills

If your student can rig and launch a boat, sail around a triangular course, come alongside or pick up a mooring or man overboard and then return safely to shore, he is competent to Level 2.

You are not concerned with perfect sail setting or boat handling, but will look for an appreciation of the five essentials and a successful negotiation of the course. You should do as much of the assessment as possible on a continuous basis, entering items in the logbook as they are completed to avoid 'exam nerves'.

Many centres conduct the final assessment in a tactful way, by treating the triangular course sessions as informal races. The syllabus therefore contains the minimum which the candidate needs to know for success on this exercise.

The aim at this level is to encourage students to continue sailing and go further in the scheme, so the certificate is awarded unless the student cannot manage the objective assessment above or is actively dangerous. Adults generally prefer oral interviews to written papers for the theory assessment of background knowledge.

## Level 3 - Improving Techniques

By this stage, the student is expected not only to negotiate a triangular course, but to sail it to best advantage in moderate winds. Look for the five essentials throughout.

It is not essential that all of the sailing techniques and manoeuvres are completed successfully, first time, but the student must understand what he should have done, why he failed and be successful on a subsequent attempt.

Most establishments have their own papers for the theory assessments. If you are asked to assess one of these, study the paper to familiarise yourself with the depth of knowledge required and ensure that you know all the answers.

## Level 4 - Racing Techniques

This is probably the most difficult course on which to give an objective assessment. The best approach is continuous assessment, with the Race Trainer ensuring that each of the techniques has been practised and understood.

## Level 5 - Advanced Skills

It is no coincidence that many of the skills covered on this course are identical to those contained in the Instructor Pre-entry Assessment, and the standard required is the same. Many of the students attending this level of course are planning to become instructors.

If the final assessment for Level 5 is conducted in enough wind by a Principal who is also an RYA Coach/Assessor, it can be entered as the Pre-entry Assessment in the log section of this book.

# ASSISTANT INSTRUCTOR TRAINING

The role of the Assistant Instructor is to assist qualified instructors to teach beginners up to the standard of the National Sailing Certificate, Level 2, and Start Sailing Stages 1, 2 and 3 of the Young Sailors Scheme. It follows that the training given should cover the teaching points related to teaching beginners, as detailed on page 39 of this book.

This training may either be given on a specific Assistant Instructor course over about 20 hours, or may be provided on a one-to-one basis over a longer period as on-the-job training. A suggested programme for a weekend course is given below, the majority of the time being spent afloat covering how to put across the various teaching points for each of the method sessions.

As this training is related directly to the work of a single teaching establishment, it follows that the emphasis is likely to be predominantly either on double handed or single handed dinghies. In providing this training, the Principal or Chief Instructor will have in his mind the role of the Assistant Instructor - helping qualified RYA Instructors. In double handed boats, the Assistant Instructor may act as helmsman in the very early stages of training, and then encourage the students to take over as soon as possible.

When teaching in single handers, the Assistant Instructor's role is that of helper, rigger, catcher, etc. The training given will reflect this.

Following training, candidates will be assessed on their practical teaching ability with beginners, according to the criteria given under Instructor Assessment in this Handbook.

| Sample programme for Assistant Instructor course | |
|---|---|
| **Friday evening** | Welcome, introductions, role of the Assistant Instructor |
| | Outline of course |
| | Basic principles of instructional technique |
| **Saturday morning** | Teaching method sessions 1 - 4 |
| **afternoon** | Teaching method sessions 5 - 7 |
| **evening** | Teaching capsize recovery and man overboard (theory) |
| **Sunday morning** | Teaching method sessions 8-11 |
| **afternoon** | Teaching method session 12 |
| | Teaching capsize recovery and man overboard (practice) |
| | Debrief |

# THE PRE-ENTRY SAILING ASSESSMENT

In order to be accepted for training at instructor level all candidates have to pass a practical test conducted by an RYA Coach/Assessor, not more than one year before instructor training. The test serves as a filter, because there is no time during the instructor course for candidates to be taught how to sail well.

It is recommended that, prior to taking the assessment, candidates satisfy themselves that they can sail a dinghy confidently to the standard detailed below and have the appropriate background knowledge.

During the assessment, which will be conducted in a minimum windspeed of 11 knots by an RYA Coach/Assessor, the candidate will be judged on his preparation for and execution of each of the tasks, including awareness of others. The assessment will be made in a boat of the candidate's choice with a Portsmouth Yardstick of less than 1230. If the assessment is conducted in a keelboat or multihull the rudderless sailing section may be omitted.

The assessment may be undertaken during a Level 5 course run by an RYA Coach/Assessor, given the minimum windspeed outlined above.

The candidate should be able to complete the following tasks, sailing at all times with an awareness of 'the Five Essentials' ie sail setting, balance, trim, centreboard and course sailed. The Assessor will be seeking to confirm that you can sail competently and confidently:

## *Sail around a triangular course*

- Each leg of the course will be a minimum of 400 metres
- Use the five essentials
- Close mark rounding
- Allow for tide if appropriate
- Use all the boat's equipment to best advantage including spinnaker if carried.

## *Sail around the same course without a rudder*

This exercise highlights your appreciation of the five essentials and demonstrates whether you understand the effects of variations in sail trim and boat balance/trim.

To a distant observer it should appear that the boat is being sailed normally with the rudder still in use. You should have no more difficulty going to windward, tacking or gybing than you did with the rudder on, although the Assessor will take the conditions into account and allow a little deviation from the ideal course.

He will expect you to make any modifications to sail area, sheeting arrangements and centreboard position before you start, so that the whole exercise proceeds smoothly. You will not be penalised for reefing the dinghy, if conditions are such that it would be seamanlike to do so. In the unlikely event of there being several boats sailing rudderless in any area, the Assessor would expect you to maintain good awareness of the other boats and take avoiding action early if necessary.

### Sail a tight circular course

- Circle less than three boat lengths' radius around a stationary (free floating) boat
- Make only one tack and one gybe
- Sail trim and boat balance/trim suited to the manoeuvre.

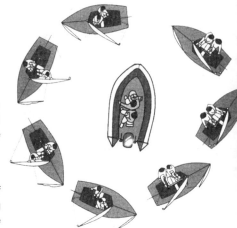

The circle should be as small as you can safely make it, but the Assessor will accept that, in doing, this, you might have to leave the centreboard in one position.

### Sail a 'follow-my-leader' course

The course may include all points of sailing and may be behind another sailing dinghy or behind a powered boat. The Assessor will be looking for a small,

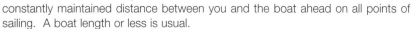

constantly maintained distance between you and the boat ahead on all points of sailing. A boat length or less is usual.

### Pick up a Man Overboard dummy

- Boat must be stopped dead in the water when you pick up the dummy
- Pick up at the windward shroud
- Do not tack while you pull it aboard
- More than one attempt should not be needed

### Demonstrate one of the following:

### Lee shore landing and departure

- Use correct sail plan (jib only if necessary)
- Land in a controlled fashion
- On departure clear the shore successfully in a controlled way on the first attempt.

### Anchor or pick up a mooring - wind against tide

- Correct sail plan
- Boat should be stopped dead next to the buoy
- Pick up buoy first time
- When mooring buoy is on board, the boat should remain under your control
- Anchoring to take place in the area designated by the Assessor
- Anchoring should be successful on the first attempt
- After the anchor has held, the boat should remain under your control.

### Come alongside a moored boat, wind against tide

- Approach under control
- Stop alongside on the first attempt
- Remain in control thereafter.

The choice of exercises above allows for pre-entry assessments being carried out in different locations. The decision as to which one is used will be made by the Assessor, who will be judging your preparation and execution of the task, including the fact that you have an escape route planned.

Throughout this section the phrase 'on the first attempt' should not be taken to mean that you cannot make a seamanlike decision to break off at a reasonably early stage and try again. It merely means that once you have become committed to a task, it should be successfully completed.

## *Recover a capsized dinghy and sail away*

You should successfully right your boat, without external help, in a calm and controlled fashion. Except in the case of gear failure you should need only one attempt. Do be prepared for this task by checking the boat (loose gear, buoyancy etc) and yourself (clothing, personal buoyancy) before the event.

Throughout the pre-entry assessment, the Assessor will try to obtain an overall impression of your sailing ability. As a result, you might technically fail one task and still pass the assessment if he feels you are up to the overall standard required of an RYA Instructor.

Just as you would not approach the driving test in a strange car without having practised reversing into a narrow opening etc, so you should not attempt the pre-entry assessment without practising all the tasks in the boat in which you intend to take the test.

Finally, please remember that although the pre-entry is likely to be conducted in a double-handed dinghy, the instructor course will include practical work in single handers. All instructors are therefore expected to be capable of sailing the single handers commonly used within teaching establishments, ie Optimist, Pico, Topper and Laser. Any Instructor candidate unfamiliar with these boats is recommended to gain some experience of them before the Instructor training course.

# THE INSTRUCTOR TRAINING COURSE

Throughout your training it is important to remember that the RYA teaching methods used have been developed successfully over many years. You will be introduced to some techniques which have become standardised because it is important that RYA instruction should follow broadly the same pattern in every teaching establishment.

It is equally important, however, that you should not follow certain drills slavishly without considering in more general terms the task which you are trying to accomplish. Without scope for minor variations, there would be no room for development and improvement.

## TEACHING BEGINNERS - LEVELS 1 AND 2

Whilst there are agreed methods for teaching virtually every aspect of our sport, the part of teaching which has become widely known as 'The Method' covers the practical techniques of basic boat handling in the Start Sailing course, Level 1.

Although this course is used on its own as a short 'taster' by many teaching establishments, it also forms the first two days of the conventional five-day beginners' course leading to the award of the Basic Skills certificate, Level 2. This is the backbone of training provided by almost every establishment.

It is perhaps because of the large numbers of students, instructors and establishments involved in this stage of teaching every year that the teaching techniques are so standardised.

This brings the great advantage that Instructors can move from one centre to another and, having first established the local 'house rules' then be perfectly at ease teaching any part of the appropriate RYA course. It also means that students can follow a course at one centre with a higher level course elsewhere, and the Instructors will know exactly what has been covered and what needs to be taught next.

The Method analyses the various elements that make up the activity of sailing a dinghy, splitting each element into simple stages. Emphasis is placed on revision and testing to ensure that each stage has been successfully learnt.

It is important for motivation that students succeed at each stage, so the pace of learning and the complexity of the task are adapted to the individual. Students are encouraged to work out solutions from basic premises supplied by the instructor. In educational terms, it is a student-centred method based on experiential learning. When teaching beginners, different establishments may use slightly different variations of the Method but all retain the basic philosophy. Thus the RYA Instructor should find no difficulty in adapting to local differences or 'house rules' within the basic framework.

The instructor course concentrates on the detail of the Method but you must never forget the overall aim - to get students sailing safely on their own as soon as possible. Each skill is broken down into easy steps for learning but, once learnt, those steps should disappear again as the manoeuvre becomes a continuous flowing action.

# FLOW DIAGRAM FOR TEACHING METHOD

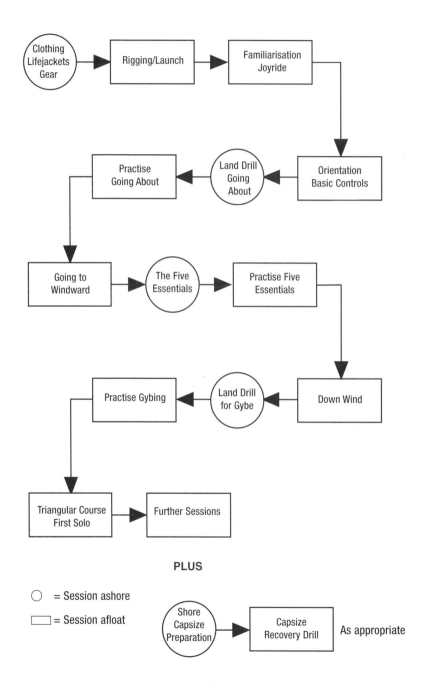

```
Clothing        →   Rigging/Launch   →   Familiarisation
Lifejackets                              Joyride
Gear
                                              ↓

Practise        ←   Land Drill       ←   Orientation
Going About         Going                Basic Controls
                    About
    ↓

Going to        →   The Five         →   Practise Five
Windward            Essentials           Essentials
                                              ↓

Practise        ←   Land Drill       ←   Down Wind
Gybing              for Gybe
    ↓

Triangular Course  →  Further Sessions
First Solo
```

**PLUS**

◯ = Session ashore

▭ = Session afloat

```
Shore           →   Capsize              As appropriate
Capsize             Recovery Drill
Preparation
```

A student who, having mastered a technique, then adapts what he has been taught to suit himself should never be criticised because he has departed from the Method for that technique. He should be encouraged to move on and learn more.

The following outline of the Teaching Method provides the sequence of sessions and the important teaching points. Your course will expand on this framework. When actually using the Method to teach beginners, some sessions may well be run together, but it is worth establishing the principle that after only 20 minutes or so the average student's ability to absorb information falls off considerably. A short break, followed by revision and informal testing, makes for much more efficient learning.

Early in your own training you will realise that the Method avoids technical terminology. Ropes, seats, push and pull are preferable to instructions which are complicated by unfamiliar terms. Your students will be having enough trouble working out what is going on without being told to 'sheet out and bear away'. Some nautical terms in common use come so naturally, however, that they will almost certainly be learnt in the first sessions.

## *Session 1. Ashore*

**Clothing/Footwear/Buoyancy aids/Gear collection**
- Warm clothing: wetsuit, drysuit, oilskins
- Footwear: wellies, trainers or sailing shoes
- Buoyancy aids: 50 Newtons, correct size, securely fastened, 150 Newtons life jackets for non-swimmers
- Gear collection: identify each item briefly

## *Session 2. Ashore or Afloat*

**Rigging/Launching**

**Rigging**
- Rig boat quickly
- Involve students
- Explain briefly
- Reef if necessary

**Launching and underway:**
- Don't waste time
- Hoist main
- Ask students and indicate wind direction

## *Session 3. Afloat*

**Familiarisation/Joyride**
- Interesting, enthusiastic and enjoyable
- Instructor at helm
- Students allocated tasks
- Students balance boat and gain awareness of wind direction
- Short session
- Calm, relaxed and controlled
- Return to shore

# Session 4.  *Afloat*
## Orientation/Basic Boat Controls

### Orientation:
- Point out landmarks and wind direction (particularly after manoeuvres such as tacking)
- Lying-to
- Figure of eight course with tack at each end
- Students take helm with target to aim at
- Instructor sits to leeward and forward of the helmsman
- Hands off the tiller
- Simple instructions such as 'pull it towards you a little'

### Demonstrate basic boat controls:
- From lying-to position pull mainsail to turn boat towards wind
- Pull jib in to turn away from wind
- Relate changes in boat direction to the direction of the wind
- Students practise
- Discreetly moving your weight may be necessary to guarantee success
- Effect of raising centreboard
- No-go-zone (the windward sector in which the sails flap)

# Session 5.  *Afloat and Ashore*
## Going About

### Land drill - going about:
- Not all students will require a land drill
- Best done on boat ashore
- Demonstrate at normal speed

### Tiller extension and aft mainsheet:

*Aft mainsheet tacking*

- Frying pan grip (palm up thumb on top)
- Spare mainsheet towards stern under the tiller
- Boat flat
- Front hand holds mainsheet
- Helmsman checks area into which he is about to sail
- Helmsman says 'Ready About'
- Crew checks and, if clear, answers 'Ready'
- Helmsman changes hands on mainsheet and tiller extension by trapping the mainsheet under thumb of rear hand and picking up tiller extension in front hand.
- Initiates turn by pushing tiller extension smoothly away from him, saying 'Lee oh' as he does it
- As boom reaches leeward quarter, crew releases jib sheet
- As boom nears centreline, helmsman starts to move across boat, facing aft and moving his front foot first
- Helmsman revolves extension away from him forward of tiller
- Crew picks up new jibsheet and balances boat.
- As boom reaches new leeward quarter, both helmsman and crew sit down

- Helmsman centralises the tiller
- Crew sheets in jib.

**Tiller extension, centre mainsheet:**
- Helmsman faces forward throughout and uses dagger grip
- Helmsman checks area into which he is going to sail
- If clear, calls 'Ready about'
- Crew uncleats jibsheet
- Crew checks area and, if on a trapeze, he moves inboard and unhooks
- When ready, he answers 'Yes'.
- Helmsman eases mainsheet slightly and calls 'Lee oh' as he pushes tiller extension firmly away
- As the boom reaches the centreline, he moves into the boat, back foot first, facing forward
- Crew starts to move across.
- Helmsman revolves extension around forward of tiller, moving across boat and still holding mainsheet in old front hand
- Crew takes up slack in new jibsheet and moves across boat.
- As sails fill, helmsman sits down on new side, steering with tiller arm behind back
- He centralises the tiller and brings sheet hand back across in front of body to hold both tiller extension and sheet, thumb pointing towards end of tiller extension. He takes mainsheet with his front hand and brings extension under arm to front of body
- Crew sheets in jib and prepares to go out on trapeze, if appropriate.
  Continue to practise until instruction not required

## *Session 6. Afloat*

**Going About Practice**

After practice the student should be able to sail around a shallow figure of eight course, going about at each end, without any help from the Instructor. Don't forget to revise and to test at the beginning of the session.
- Tack from reach to reach often
- Ensure boat is going fast enough to tack
- Check crew and jib position
- Repeat shore drill if necessary

## *Session 7. Afloat*

**Going to Windward**

In fluctuating winds, sailing on a close reach initially will make life easier for your students if it avoids being headed by windshifts.
- Demonstrate that the sails flap as boat turns towards the wind
- Demonstrate the No-go-zone again
- Explain the concept of beating to windward
- Take the boat downwind
- Hand over to the student and ask to be sailed to a point directly upwind

Many students will now be able to do this unaided so only intervene if you feel that it is really necessary.

- Don't worry if the tacking is inefficient
- Use the flapping of the jib luff as an indicator of the edge of the No-go-zone
- Relate progress to landmarks
- Check ability to determine wind direction
- Stress that the angle between the sails and the wind stays the same wherever the boat is pointing.

## Session 8.  Ashore and Afloat

### The Five Essentials

### 1 Sail Setting

- Restate the point regarding the angle between the sails and the wind
- Simple board sketch or a working model
- Sails should be 'just not flapping'
- Ease sails when turning away from the wind and sheet in when turning towards the wind (which will also aid tacking)
- One of the most common faults at this stage is the failure to sheet out when bearing away.

### 2 Balance

- Sail upright for minimum drag
- Demonstrate afloat how heeling makes the boat turn
- Every rudder movement slows the boat.

### 3 Trim

- Show trim for different points of sailing.
- Explain why the boat goes better close hauled with weight forward

### 4 Centreboard

- Demonstrate levels for different points of sailing

### 5 Course sailed

- Explain different courses that will take you to windward
- If the students are ready, introduce the idea that one course may be better than another because of tide, wind shadows or hazards - all in a very basic form
- Encourage students to make their own decisions based on personal observation.

## Session 9.  Afloat

### Downwind

- Revise and test all previous work
- Demonstrate the action of the jib as the training run turns into a dead run
- Allow plenty of room (wind against tide is ideal)
- Students practise running,  turning from a beam reach, through a broad reach to a training run and then back to close-hauled
- Any change in direction requires changes in the Five Essentials
- Avoid gybing but also avoid horror stories about it

- End this session with a smooth controlled demonstration gybe.

## *Session 10. Ashore*

### Shore Drills for Gybing

- Explain fundamental difference between tacking and gybing
- Take the fear out of gybing
- Stress the very clear difference in commands - 'Ready About' for tacking but 'Stand by to Gybe' for gybing which avoids any possible confusion.

*Training run*

### Tiller extension, aft mainsheet:

- Helmsman sits forward of the tiller and puts the boat on a training run
- He checks inside the boat, particularly to see that the centreboard is only slightly down
- He checks around the boat, especially the area into which he is going to sail and says 'Stand by to gybe'
- Crew checks the area and says 'Yes'
- Helmsman pulls in mainsheet to bring boom clear of shroud
- He changes hands on mainsheet and tiller extension
- He says 'Gybe oh' and moves towards middle of boat, taking tiller extension round and forward towards the other side
- Demonstrate that, before the gybe, the extension swings right around the end of the tiller without the tiller itself being moved.
- Helmsman initiates gybe by pushing the tiller extension towards where he was sitting and waits for the boom to swing across
- As the mainsail clew lifts, the helmsman quickly centralises the tiller so that his weight, the boom and the tiller are simultaneously in the middle of the boat
- Crew changes jibsheets and moves to centre of boat.
- He sits out on the new windward side
- Crew balances the boat and sets the jib once it has changed sides.

### Tiller Extension, centre mainsheet:

The important difference about this drill is that the helmsman takes hold of the falls of the mainsheet to guide the boom across, preventing a violent gybe.

- Helmsman balances boat as necessary and checks all round - especially area into which boat is turning
- He holds extension in dagger grip and calls 'Stand by to gybe'
- Crew checks area and says 'Yes'
- Helmsman steps back foot first into the middle of the boat whilst revolving extension over to new side without altering tiller itself
- Helmsman holds falls of mainsheet
- Crew moves into centre of boat and changes jib sheets.
- Helmsman calls 'Gybe Oh', pushes tiller towards original sitting position and guides boom across with falls
- As soon as boom starts to move, he centralises tiller and sits down on new windward side
- Crew balances boat.

- Helmsman brings sheet hand back across in front of body to hold both tiller extension and sheet, thumb pointing towards end of tiller extension. He takes the mainsheet with his front hand and brings extension under arm to front of body
- He trims mainsheet and settles down on new course
- Crew trims jibsheet.

## Session 11.  Afloat

**Gybing Practice**
- Consider reefing
- Allow plenty of room (wind against tide if possible)
- Stay calm

## Session 12.  Afloat

**Triangular course /First solo**
- Triangular course: lay course with one leg to windward
- Sail with students and then move into the teaching boat
- Give instruction where necessary but avoid shouting from the teaching boat, bring students alongside if necessary
- Remember you are still responsible for the safety of boat and crew

## Further sessions

In the course of the previous sessions students will have left and returned to base on several occasions.  They can now go on to learn jetty work, man overboard, picking up moorings, coming alongside a moored boat etc with more intensity. You will be in and out of the dinghy, demonstrating particular skills and then watching progress from the shore or an escort boat.  When setting courses for students, remember that you need to be able to communicate with them throughout using some of the skills explained in the single handers section.

Awareness of other boats will have been part of your teaching in the early stages.  Stress it again now.  Discuss 'Rule of the Road' problems as they occur and your solo crew will be less likely to become involved in collisions.

## Capsize Recovery Drill

Capsize recovery drill will fit into your programme at the earliest practical moment.  Weather, water temperature and other considerations will influence your Senior Instructor's decision, but it is generally agreed that early capsizing is beneficial.

The end of a day's sailing provides the best opportunities for drying clothes, personal buoyancy and gear.  Students are usually apprehensive about the capsize, and that apprehension can blunt the fine edge of their ability to learn.  Once capsizing is over, they learn quickly and are less worried.  You can also send them solo with a clearer conscience.

As an instructor, your responsibility is always to go into the water with your students during capsize drill.  Right up to this stage, you have been teaching in close proximity to your students and it would seem strange if you now left them to fend for themselves.  You cannot adequately control the drill from the escort boat, although it should, of course, be standing by. The drill must go smoothly and calmly to have the desired effect of building confidence.

- Always ensure that sufficient rescue cover is provided
- Shore briefing or drill using a dinghy tipped on its side
- Explain the scoop method
- Check personal and boat buoyancy
- Check students (contact lenses, glasses, watches and even false teeth!)
- Consider buoying the top of the mast if your boat inverts easily
- Your Senior Instructor is responsible for selecting a suitable site for the drill, away from hazards but close enough to base for safety and recovery
- You are responsible for tipping the boat over (wild swinging on the shrouds is unnecessary: a brisk tack with the mainsail sheeted well in and the crew staying on the old windward side of the boat should cause a gentle capsize
- Smile, stay calm
- Direct operations from the bow of the boat so you can see both the person on the centreboard and the crew inside the boat
- Keep encouraging students but keep your physical assistance to a minimum
- The students will be much more confident if they have righted the dinghy without your help

Repeat capsize until each student has succeeded but watch out for exhaustion or hypothermia problems after two or three attempts. It is better to stow the boat and gear after everyone has changed rather than risk difficulties with the cold. Maintain constant encouragement.

The six steps of the Scoop Method outlined in RYA book G3 for an aft-mainsheet dinghy are repeated here in order to stress certain specific teaching points associated with each.

**Step 1**
- Both the crew swim to the stern
- Helmsman checks that the rudder is secure and not floating off
- Crew finds the end of the mainsheet and gives it to the helmsman who, using it as a lifeline, swims around the outside of the boat to the centreboard
- Crew then swims along the inside of the boat to the centreboard case.

Following initial immersion, most students are still regaining their breath by the time the helmsman has to go UNDER the mainsheet assembly to get clear round to the centreboard. Many try to swim over the top and some get their personal buoyancy hooked into the various floating bits of rope. Warn them of these difficulties.

**Step 2**
- The crew checks that the centreboard is fully down
- Helmsman holds onto it to prevent the boat inverting.

If the centreboard is not fully down, warn the crew of the risk of injury to the helmsman from an over-enthusiastic attempt to lower it without warning.

**Step 3**
- Crew finds the top (weather) jib sheet and throws it over to the helmsman
- Helmsman confirms that he has it.

Confirmation of receipt is often inaudible, especially if the helmsman has failed to achieve it. The centreboard case is a useful slot through which to shout.

**Step 4**

Crew lies in the hull facing forwards and floats above the side-deck, being sure not to hang on (his extra weight won't help the helmsman and indeed might make it impossible for the helmsman to right the dinghy).

Many students do not, initially, realise the great importance of this point. Some even disregard it, believing that they will be safer by hanging on.

**Step 5**

- Helmsman preferably lies back straight in the water with his feet on the boat's gunwale and hauls on the jibsheet
- Alternatively he climbs onto the centreboard, keeping his weight as close to the hull as possible to avoid breaking the board, and hauls on the jibsheet to right the dinghy with the crew member in it.

Some find it difficult to get onto the centreboard. Any preliminary advice which you can provide is worth giving. Heavyweights will be able to right the dinghy by the first method. With lightweights, the advice to keep as close to the hull as possible has to be modified in practice, as their weight is sometimes insufficient to provide the necessary righting moment. Stress the value of straight legs and back for maximum leverage.

**Step 6**

- With the jib backed the dinghy is hove-to and the crew is then able to help the helmsman aboard
- Helmsman may find that he can get halfway into the boat as it comes upright.

The right place for the helmsman to be brought aboard is beside the weather shroud. Discuss the option of rolling the boat to windward if you have a lightweight crew and a heavyweight helmsman.

## *Man Overboard Recovery*

Use dummy (fender and tyre) not a real person.

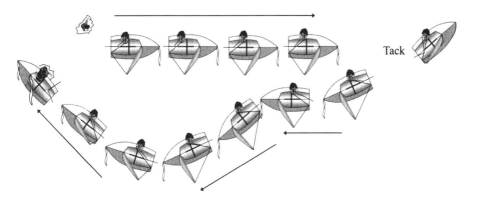

- Regain control immediately and turn onto a beam reach
- Maintain visual contact
- Sail away on beam to broad reach for 10 boat lengths, or enough to get the boat under control
- Tack and point the boat at the MOB. Check the main will flap
- Bear away slightly if necessary so that final approach is on a close reach
- Spill and fill the mainsail to control boatspeed
- Stop to leeward of a MOB
- Helmsman goes forward and retrieves the MOB by the windward shroud
- A flick to windward on the tiller helps prevent the boat tacking on top of the MOB, who will act as a drogue or sea anchor to keep the dinghy in the basic hove-to position
- Repeat with helmsman as MOB, ie crew takes control of the boat.

If it happened for real, the MOB should shout or whistle to gain attention but not swim about or he will rapidly lose body heat. If wearing personal buoyancy with additional oral inflation, he should inflate it, although it may need to be deflated for boarding.

Outline the aftercare needed for a real casualty.

Once your students have mastered the basic principles, encourage more realistic practice by briefing them that it should be the helmsman who 'falls overboard'. When the dummy is dropped over the side, the helmsman should let go of the tiller and mainsheet, move out of the way of the crew and take no further part in the manoeuvre. This results in the crew having to regain full control of the dinghy and achieves better results.

## *Further practical sessions*

### Coming alongside a moored boat or jetty/picking up a mooring
- Choose approach line and escape route
- Ensure sails will flap
- Drop mainsail if wind against or across tide
- Communication with crew

### Teaching racing - Level 2

As you will see later, the end of a typical Level 2 course is marked by a practical assessment in which the students sail around a triangular course. Many establishments complete the Level 2 course by organising a short informal race, thus encouraging students to consolidate their skills and introducing them to the competitive side of the sport. Assuming that you have covered the basic rules of the road, the minimum extra knowledge needed by students to complete this satisfactorily is an explanation of the typical port-hand triangular course and a basic starting procedure.

# TEACHING LEVEL 3

## Manoeuvres

Many of these are a revision and refinement of skills learnt on a Level 2 course. Each technique can be broken down into four stages:

- Planning
- Approach
- Manoeuvre
- Escape

A briefing and demonstration or land drill ashore can be used for many techniques.

Practice doesn't necessarily make perfect - it may serve only to repeat poor technique and hence reinforce mistakes. That's where you come in.

Don't simply leave your students afloat to practise their anchoring or reefing all afternoon while you lounge in the teaching boat or ashore. Provide goals for their performance by setting precise areas in which to anchor and make the target progressively smaller.

Give an incentive for a good reef by requiring the students to sail to windward after taking it in. Provide goals for good lee shore landings or alongside practice by having prizes on the beach or jetty.

Ideally, bring all the manoeuvres together once they have been learnt into the framework of a seamanship exercise or, if you want to make it competitive, a seamanship game.

The principle is just that you combine the exercises in a way which will make their practice more enjoyable and their execution more efficient. The golden rule about such games is to keep them simple. As soon as you get bogged down in penalty points and the like, the fun will evaporate.

If, on the other hand, the game is packaged properly, your students won't have time to realise that you are simply providing structured practice. It could be marketed as an obstacle course or treasure hunt full of local interest.

## Working from a teaching boat

With many of the topics outlined above, the instructor may first be in the sailing dinghy, but then is most likely to be out of it, allowing the students to practise under supervision. As soon as you get out of the dinghy your communication problems increase. Read the section on communication later in the chapter on single handers (see page 52).

One further tip might be useful when teaching spinnaker work. Once you have moved from the land drill, spinnaker practice can take up a lot of searoom. Reduce it - and the communication problem - by getting your students to tow your teaching boats while practising their hoist and gybes. On tidal water, programme the session, if possible, when the wind is against the tide.

## Reefing afloat

- When to reef - purpose
- Where to reef - away from hazards, starboard tack if possible
- How - order of events, co-ordination between helm and crew

- How much - appearance of reefed sail, ie efficient shape, boom not drooped, no wrinkles, kicking strap still effective
- Genoa changed to jib and centreboard raised slightly if necessary.

## *Anchoring*

**Briefing ashore - Type of anchor and selection of suitable anchorage**
- Nature of bottom
- Shelter
- Depth (changes with tide)
- Length of warp

**Afloat**
- Approach on close reach or against tidal stream
- Drop main if wind against tide
- Lower anchor when boat stops
- Pay out warp
- Check holding with transits
- Stow sails.

## *Towing*
- Good communication
- Approach (another dinghy or powerboat)
- Pass tow line
- Drop mainsail
- Secure towline
- Bridle/strongpoints
- Quick release system
- Towing alongside
- Springs
- Towing stern first
- Being towed
- Centreboard up
- Crew weight aft
- Steer if possible.

## *Spinnaker if carried*
See Advanced Instructor training, page 78

# THE USE OF POWERED CRAFT IN A TEACHING ENVIRONMENT

Part of the skill of a dinghy instructor is to be able to teach from a powerboat, which is why Level 2 is a pre-requisite for dinghy instructors.

- Don't shout from a moving powerboat to a moving dinghy
- Tell the students to stop and lie-to
- Approach the dinghy slowly from the windward side
- Keep the prop away from people and ropes
- A capsized boat should always be approached bow to (techniques are given in G16 Safety Boat Handbook)
- Take care when approaching the shore to keep clear of people in the water and avoid damage to the prop

The Level 2 course will include a knowledge of the basic equipment required. The sailing instructor should add to this as necessary.

# TEACHING TECHNIQUES USING SINGLE HANDED DINGHIES

It is no accident that single handers are so popular in teaching establishments - and in the sport of dinghy sailing. Students are in control of their own boat right from the start. They are continuously at the helm and so cannot fail to benefit by practising new techniques and learning immediately from their mistakes. The boats themselves are simple, light and exciting to sail.

## *General points*

### Advantages
- Students continuously at the helm
- They learn faster
- Light
- Simple and exciting
- Particularly effective for teaching children
- Inexpensive to run
- Durable

### Problems
- Can be frustrating at first
- Students tire easily
- Communication is harder
- Group control
- Cold quicker

You will be responsible for up to six students, possibly well scattered, at one time. Also, because students are always at the helm, possibly in lively boats, they will become tired more quickly.

Sessions should therefore be short and the instructor must always watch for signs of fatigue. Capsize is more likely in a singlehander than in the instructed larger dinghy, so suitable preparation must be made, as outlined below.

## *Environment*

It is important to put your students in the right environment to achieve the tasks required.

### Look at
- Equipment - the right size of boat and sail area for the size of student
- Wind strength
- Wind direction
- Temperature
- Sailing area
- Depth of water
- Starting point (beach/pontoon/lake bank/slipway etc)
- Length of sessions (short)

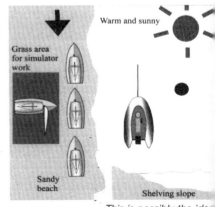

Warm and sunny

Grass area for simulator work

Sandy beach

Shelving slope

*This is possibly the idea sailing venu*

## Group control
- Frequent briefings
- Recall signals (whistle and hand signals)
- Awareness of sailing area- diagrams, set course before students go afloat so they can see the boundaries
- Question students to check understanding
- Size of sailing area
- Use of 'buddy' system at first sessions

## What if....?
**Always consider**
- What is the worst thing that could happen?
- What changes can you make to cope with this?

## Communication
- Well thought out and structured briefings (include problems that might occur)
- Size of sailing area
- You should not have to shout to your students
- Students stop the boat and you go to them, or students come to you
- Be aware of the noise from an engine or a sail flapping
- If possible take a spare dinghy and sail with your students
- If students can see tasks they will pick them up quicker than simply being told
- Keep session short
- Good debrief

## Capsize
Because your students are on their own and not very confident, you must point out:
- Righting a boat is easy
- It can be fun
- Wearing the right equipment means they will float in the water
- Demonstration from instructor first to show how easy it is
  Even on a hot sunny day your students can get cold, once wet:
- Try to avoid capsize practice until the end of the day
- Try to keep them as dry as possible (consider reefing)
- Land drill where possible

## Philosophy
The basic philosophy of the RYA Teaching Method outlined earlier applies just as much to single handed teaching as to conventional techniques, but at any stage you should ask yourself two questions:
- What do students already know?
- What is the minimum they need to know before they can complete the next session successfully?

This should save you unnecessary time ashore and save you teaching irrelevant details.

## OUTLINE PROGRAMME FOR SINGLEHANDERS

The programme given below is just one of many which have been developed successfully. It is not intended to be definitive, merely to provide an introduction to the techniques needed.

Think of the timing of your shore sessions. You have to cover a lot before going afloat.

### Session 1. Ashore

**Clothing/footwear/personal buoyancy/gear collection**
- As for basic Method
- Consider drysuits and helmets
- Buoyancy aids are preferred to lifejackets

### Session 2. Ashore

**Rigging**
- Reinforce wind direction
- Rig one boat first as a demonstration
- Students can rig their own boats
- Check each one before they go afloat

### Session 3. Ashore

**Tacking land drill/getting out of irons**
- Demonstrate going about
- Reinforce wind direction
- Swing boat through the wind
- Demonstrate tacking using the method (centre main or aft mainsheet)
- Each student should then practise
- Demonstrate getting out of irons (push/push, pull/pull)

### Session 4. Afloat

**Practise tacking/Beam reach/Starting and stopping**
- Boats rigged
- Demonstrate launching one boat
- Instructor demonstrates what is to be done
- Instructor in the water
- Check student's orientation is correct
- Before letting go, go through sailing position, starting and stopping, tacking (walk boat through tack)
- Once ready send off on way to buoy
- Talk student through tack
- Talk student back to you, stopping the boat by you

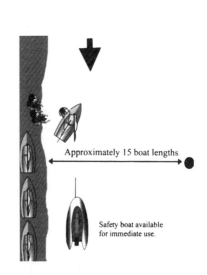

Approximately 15 boat lengths

Safety boat available for immediate use.

- Once each student has had a go, set up a beam reach figure of eight course

## *Session 5. Ashore and afloat*

**Turning towards and away from the wind**
- Lay course as shown
- Move buoy further into wind as session continues
- Brief clearly using board or diagram
- Demonstrate ashore or afloat the sail positions as boat turns towards and away from the wind
- Reinforce wind direction at each step
- Use four steps for getting from beam reach to close hauled
- Students practise
- Go afloat one boat at a time to revise session 4.
- Move buoy up in stages
- Debrief ashore at end of session.

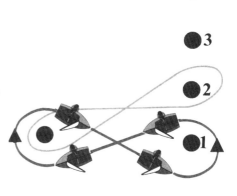

## *Session 6. Ashore and afloat*

**Going to windward**
- Lay course as shown
- Brief clearly using board or diagram
- Reinforce no-go-zone
- Demonstrate in water or on simulator, effects on sail
- Revise luffing up and bearing away
- Demonstrate
- Send off students one at a time at intervals
- Introduce the Five Essentials to this exercise

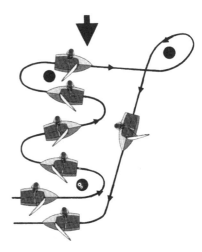

## Session 7. Ashore and afloat

### Gybing practice
- Demonstrate on land using the method (centre main/aft main)
- Training run
- Daggerboard position
- Reinforce Five Essentials
- Allow each student to practise

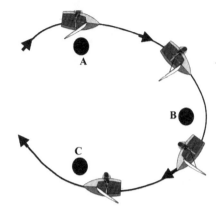

## Session 8. Afloat

### Triangular Course
- Lay course as shown
- Demonstrate to students
- Send students off one at a time at intervals
- Move mark B until AB and BC become training runs
- Avoid dead runs and death rolls caused by sailing by the lee
- Debrief ashore

## General comments
- Keep sessions short and intensive
- Clear briefings are essential
- Debrief each session
- Lay marks between sessions so your students can see the course before setting off
- Check equipment before the course begins

In ideal conditions, with above average students and good support, Sessions 1 to 8 can be completed in a single long day. It is far more practical, however, to treat this as two days of instruction, which is the usual time taken for an RYA Level 1 course.

Single handers are particularly appropriate for teaching children.

## Further sessions

### Coming alongside
- Same principles apply.
- Can only be achieved in wind against tide conditions by releasing the mainsail completely or releasing the clew

### Lee shore landings
- Explain when to raise daggerboard and rudder and when to ease kicker
- Release clew as soon as possible before recovery

Manoeuvres such as collecting objects in the water, using the MOB technique and sailing up to moorings are good boat handling practice.

If your students are working towards their Level 2 certificate, you now have several days to consolidate the basic techniques and cover the onshore teaching and jetty work etc afloat.

You will already have used a number of buoys to establish short courses for the early sessions. Introduce students to the slalom course, which is an ideal compact way of encouraging tacking and gybing practise. Guidance on how to make up and lay a slalom is given in the section on Mark laying (page 59).

The following are games to reinforce sailing skills taken from the NSSA's publication 'Sailing Across the Curriculum'.

### Duck Hunt Catch

With the group afloat or awaiting a Le Mans start on the whistle, the 'ducks' are spread over the sailing area. The winner is the person or team to collect the greatest number.

Variation: Award points by 'duck' colour, size or marking. The winner is still the one with the highest score but this offers a more tactical game.

Teaching points: Going about, gybing, awareness of other boats, avoiding collisions.

Resources: Plastic containers/half inflated balloons containing a little water to stop them blowing away.

### Orienteering afloat

As for land orienteering by using buoys marked with code letters.

Teaching points: sailing on all points of the wind.

Resources: Buoys, coloured or marked with code letters.

### Tag

One boat is 'it', raises dagger board half way, throws tennis ball at other boats. If it hits, then struck boat is 'it', retrieves tennis ball, raises dagger board half-way and chases other boats. Useful to play when using different types of boats - Oppies and Toppers.

Teaching points: Use of centre/dagger board, speed control.

Resources: Tennis ball, large buoyant sponge, buoyant frisbee.

### Relays

Team event to transport baton/piece of equipment/person from one shore to another.

Variations: transport to a boat, race round a slalom course, collect gear required for a task. All of these need very clear instructions about changeover procedures, what and how objects can be carried, time penalties etc.

Teaching points: sailing accurately on all points of sailing, landing on lee shore, leaving lee shore.

Resources: Buckets, tennis balls, corks

## Rounders

This is not a team game, each boat tries to beat the scores of all the other boats. In turn, all boats come alongside the anchored rescue boat - the base. The 'batting' boat throws a ball in any direction and then sails around the buoys. Each buoy rounded scores a rounder. Fielding boats retrieve balls and either hit the batting boat or return the ball to base.

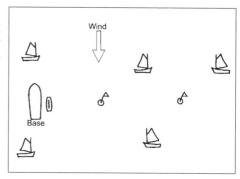

Teaching points: reaching, coming alongside

Resources: one tennis ball, 4 to 6 boats

## Topper race all standing

Race around a triangular course without sitting down in the boat (tack either by walking around the mast or by stepping between boom and sail foot; gybe by stepping around sail clew.

Teaching points: Boat balance and trim

Resources: Three buoys

## Treasure Hunt

Mix clues both onshore and on-the-water. Have each team follow a completely different order of clues. End with a picnic or barbecue when the 'treasure' is discovered. (Have some treasure for everyone, not just the first team). Add to the fun with pirate costumes!

Teaching points: Accurate and fast sailing, team building.

Resources: Laminated clue sheets, face paints, box of dressing up clothes, 'treasure'.

## More advanced techniques

The majority of teaching in singlehanders is aimed at beginners, covering Levels 1 and 2 of the RYA National Sailing Scheme. Much of the content of Level 3 courses - concerned with traditional boat handling skills - is inappropriate to singlehanders but the same cannot be said for Level 4 - Racing Techniques.

Singlehanders are popular for teaching many aspects of the Level 4 course, as their simplicity of handling allows helmsmen to concentrate on learning and practising the skills of strategy and tactics. Just as we have a fairly stylised pattern for training beginners, so there is a standard set of race training exercises used by RYA Race Trainers.

An outline of the Race Trainers course is given on page 64, but please don't assume that the exercises outlined are appropriate only to race training. Many are concerned with improving boat handling techniques and as such are valuable to all students who have mastered the basic skills of sailing.

### Conclusion

Try to maintain an atmosphere of controlled excitement during training. The boats are exciting in themselves but it is up to you to keep the students occupied and learning all the time.

Remember that the programme above is just one of many which have been developed successfully over the years. Another aimed specifically at younger children is outlined in the Club Guide. Although children may be more adept at developing new skills, their attention span may be much shorter and so the same techniques are covered over a longer period, interspersed with other activities.

There is no single 'right' way; each club or centre will develop its own programme best suited to its needs. All, however, will follow the same broad philosophy of training.

## MARK LAYING FOR SHORT COURSES

When running singlehanded, improvers or racing sessions, you will need to lay a succession of short, easily moved courses. To avoid problems, remember the following points:

- Keep marks as simple as possible.
- Avoid complicated systems with blocks and weights. Sinkers are cheaper and less trouble than anchors.
- Always lay marks over the windward side of your teaching boat.
- Have the warp flaked ready, with the sinker on top ready to go.
- Retrieve marks in the same way.
- Reflake neatly as you haul in.
- Lay a warp only just longer than the depth of water.
- Don't use warps which float (polypropylene).
- A range of marks of different colours makes identification easier.
- Carry a burgee or wind indicator as an aid to laying accurate courses relative to the wind.
- Carry a compass to aid laying precise course angles.
- It is sometimes easier to lay a mark in approximately the right place, then tow it into its exact position. Sinkers make this easier than anchors.
- Have a simple communication system if working with a mother ship or committee boat.
- Don't be afraid to move a course after large windshifts.

### Slalom courses

Every teaching establishment should have access to a simple slalom course, which can be used by almost every group of students for concentrated practice. The most rudimentary system is simply a number of buoys, laid individually, each with their own sinker.

Laying this requires considerable work, especially in deep water, and means even more work after large windshifts. It is far better to make up a linked system using a long groundline and a number of risers, each one with a buoy.

In non-tidal waters each groundline needs only one anchor, laid at the windward end of the slalom, but in wind against tide or wind across tide conditions, the groundline will have to be anchored at each end.

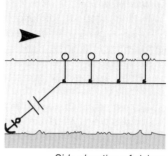

*Side elevation of slalom*

The length of each riser need only be slightly greater than the maximum draught of your fleet (including the teaching boat), with a small weight at the bottom to keep the riser vertical and the groundline low. A quick release system for attaching risers to the groundline makes it easier to modify the slalom - altering the distance between buoys according to weather conditions, students' abilities and the type of training.

The most common arrangement for slalom buoys is shown in the diagram. It can be used as a 'funnel' for repeated tacking, with the wing mark set to keep boats clear of the slalom when heading back to the start.

Exactly the same layout serves for downwind practice, but the intention here is that students should gybe around each buoy in turn. It is conventional to put the wing mark on the

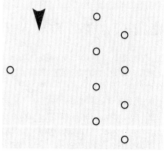

*Plan view of slalom*

starboard side of the course this time, in order that students will be approaching the top of the slalom on starboard tack.

To lay this course you will need two of the downwind strings of buoys described above, together with the isolated wing mark. It takes a certain finesse to get the mark spacing correct relative to the students' abilities.

It is impossible to be dogmatic about how many boatlengths' separation are needed for different abilities - it's probably better to define the spacing as enough to allow the student to recover from the manoeuvre of rounding one buoy, settle down and plan the next rounding before he has to do it.

Anything less than about four boat lengths is going to be counter-productive even for the most experienced sailor, as the boat will have to be thrown into the manoeuvres without any planning or style.

If the double string is too complicated, you can still achieve a great deal with a single slalom line. All it takes is a little more self-discipline by the student to ensure that he does tack or gybe at each buoy as appropriate.

By alternating the colours of the buoys in each string, you can build in different levels of ability; stage one is simply to use all the buoys of one colour; stage two is to use all the buoys.

The final development is to lay a slalom consisting of a double string narrowing down to a single string, with the spacing getting progressively narrower.

# THE INSTRUCTOR COURSE ASSESSMENT

Following the five days of your Instructor training, your course will be moderated by an RYA Coach/Assessor to confirm whether you match up to the qualities of an RYA Instructor outlined at the beginning of this handbook.

Conventionally, the assessment will take place immediately after the training course, but there are some advantages in delaying it until you have had time to put all the theory of instructional technique into practice. If your training Coach feels that you are not yet ready for assessment immediately after training, he will probably recommend that you wait until you have brushed up on some of your techniques or gained more confidence from assisting qualified instructors.

Before the assessment starts, the Assessor will agree with you a plan for the day, so that you can show evidence of your competence in instructional ability afloat and ashore. The specific items involved in the assessment are: practical instruction afloat, a prepared teaching activity, shore drills and written paper, although for convenience the paper may have been given during the training course.

If you feel slightly apprehensive about the assessment, try to think of the Assessor as both a detective and a judge. You stand accused of being a competent instructor - the Assessor's job is to gather enough evidence to get a conviction! In other words, you should be working together to ensure that your ability exceeds the minimum standard set, so that in turn students on RYA courses can be sure of receiving accurate instruction in a safe, enjoyable environment.

## *Practical instruction based on RYA teaching methods*

Whenever possible, this will be done with beginners. The usual arrangement is for a group of people to be brought in specifically for you to teach, and it is very important that they are properly briefed on their role.

It is also likely that the Assessor will have to play the part of a beginner or an improver at some stage in the assessment, so that he can test your teaching over a range of skills properly. When this happens, he will explain the role he is going to play and the stage of ability which he has reached. If you are in any doubt about his briefing, please ask him to explain further.

**The Assessor will be looking for:**
- The ability to plan the session according to the needs of your students.
- A friendly, supportive manner towards your students, from their arrival to departure.
- The boat rigged according to weather conditions and the abilities of your students.
- Adequate boat control at all times.
- Teaching according to the methods outlined on your course and in this booklet, progressing according to the students' abilities.
- Correct positioning of instructor and students.
- Successful demonstrations and clear explanations.
- Correct diagnosis and tactful correction of students' faults.
- Use of lying-to position for crew changes and briefings.

It is far more natural for you to be teaching beginners than for another instructor or the Assessor to play the role of a student, but if the latter is necessary the Assessor will take account of the false situation.

When beginners are used, the Assessor will also be assessing you through their reaction, looking for the three key factors which are important for successful teaching:

- Are the students safe?
- Are they learning anything valuable?
- Are they enjoying themselves?

No particular weighting is put on any one of these three, as they are inter-related. The good instructor is the one who meets each of these goals all the time.

## *Prepared 10 minute talk/training activity*

The Assessor will not expect you to be a professional lecturer or a polished orator; in fact the title of this part of the assessment is deliberately chosen to allow a practical bias. He will be looking for the following:

- Overall format clear - introduction, development and summary
- Audible, interesting voice - right speed of presentation
- Accurate, relevant content - sufficient material but not way beyond the demands of the syllabus
- Essential points emphasised and summarised
- Teaching aids prepared and used as appropriate
- Difficulties discovered and explained
- Questions prompted and answered

The most common faults of nervous, inexperienced instructors are to try to cram too much detail into the time available and then rush through it by speaking too quickly. During your preparation, remember to split the content up into:

- What must be covered
- What should be covered
- What could be covered

Then rehearse to see how it fits into the time available. You can then edit the talk by cutting out or shortening some of the less important detail.

## *Practical demonstration of shore drills*

The assessor may expect you to cover tiller extension drills for aft and/or centre mainsheet dinghies. Before doing so, he will have discussed with your training Coach the techniques used during the course, in case there are any local differences from the drills outlined in this handbook.

The Assessor is not trying to catch you out by minute attention to detail, but he will be looking for:

- A brief explanation of why drills are used
- Adequate preparation (and explanation) of equipment
- Good positioning of students
- Clear accurate demonstrations at normal speed and slowly with commentary
- Ability to identify and correct students' faults

## The written paper

Although the written paper forms part of your assessment as an RYA Instructor, it is included under the 'training' part of the course as a practical necessity. It is difficult enough for the visiting Assessor to conduct all the practical parts of the assessment in one day, let alone invigilate and mark a written paper.

Conventionally, it will be scheduled into the programme towards the end of the course, and it is designed with two objectives in mind. The first is to confirm that there are no large gaps in the background knowledge of the subjects you are intending to teach; the second is to provide an assessment of those areas of teaching which cannot realistically be covered by practical assessment.

Literary or artistic excellence is not required, but you will have to prove that you understand both the facts and how best to put them across.

## Overall assessment

It is usual for a number of candidates to be assessed on the same day and this will result in some time when you are not directly under the attention of the Assessor, but he may still be keeping a distant eye on your work.

Throughout the assessment, in addition to considering the detailed points outlined above, the Assessor will be making an overall (or holistic) judgement, based on the criteria and measured against his experience of the sport. The qualities sought can be summarised as:

- Enthusiasm for the sport
- Confidence in the subject
- Teaching ability
- Awareness
- Anticipation

At some point, often at the middle of the day, he will seek comments from the training Coach, who has been monitoring your progress throughout the course and so has a good idea of your ability. This will help the Assessor to take account of any particular circumstances on the day.

The Assessor and training coach will review your performance with you. This debrief may include several more questions, to ensure that you have sufficient understanding of different aspects of work as an instructor.

Finally, the training coach and Assessor will confirm whether or not you have yet proved your competence as an RYA Dinghy Instructor, complete the necessary paperwork and agree an action plan with you for the future. Such a plan will help you to overcome any gaps in your knowledge or ability, if for some reason you are not entirely successful in the assessment.

If you disagree with the decision, he will discuss the way in which you can be reassessed by someone else, or the procedure for appeal to the RYA.

# RYA RACE TRAINING

The aim of the RYA Race Training Scheme is to provide a framework where each active racing club or class association has a Club Racing Coach or RYA Racing Coach in order to convert recreational sailors into racers at club level so that existing keen competitors can quickly improve their skills.

Details of the role, eligibility, training and assessment for RYA Club Racing Coaches and RYA Racing Coaches are given earlier in this book, while the overall structure of the scheme is outlined in the table below.

## THE COACHING SCHEME FOR RACE TRAINING

| Youth | Adult | COACHED BY | TRAINED BY |
|---|---|---|---|
| UK Youth Teams | International/ Olympic Team training | National Racing Coaches | RYA/ National Coaching Foundation |
| Winter training  Blue Badge (Advanced) | Class Association training | Racing Coaches | National Racing Coaches |
| White Badge (Intermediate)  Red Badge (Introductory) | Introductory Race Training | Race Trainers | Regional Race Training Co-ordinators |

### Youth Race Training - RYA Young Sailors Scheme

Full details of the Red, White and Blue Badges of the Young Sailors Scheme are published in the G11 logbook.

### Adult Race Training

This scheme has two main objectives; to introduce competent sailors to club racing and then to provide a structured learning and coaching programme in order that active helmsmen and crews may quickly improve their racing skills.

Level 4 Introductory racing courses are run by sailing clubs for their members, and by RYA Recognised Teaching Establishments for the public. The aim of these short courses is to teach the basic principles of current racing practice to proficient sailors so that they can participate in and enjoy club racing. The detailed syllabus of the course is given in G4.

Racing clinics are normally run by Class Associations for a specific type of boat. They are usually run on a national basis though some of the larger classes run regional courses. These clinics are intended for good club sailors, with the aim of improving their performance for open meetings and regattas.

Most of the popular International Class Associations run high level "squad" training for their international teams. This class-specific training is normally tailored towards preparation for a particular European or World championship.

# RYA RACING CLINICS

## Aim

To improve the racing skills and knowledge of experienced club racers and open meeting sailors.

## Experience

A minimum of two years regular club racing incorporating some open meeting/ regatta experience.

## Format

These clinics are class specific and are normally organised by class associations typically over a weekend. The programme is planned taking into account the requirements of the sailors from the list of topics suggested below.

Practical topics are taught using race training exercises or short races preceded by thorough briefings and followed by careful analysis and discussion.

Expert speakers may cover more theoretical subjects in the form of lectures.

## Taught by

Racing Coaches familiar with the class or their specialist subject e.g: racing rules, meteorology.

# INTERNATIONAL TEAM TRAINING

## Aim

To prepare representative teams for major international regattas.

## Experience

Highly accomplished racing sailors selected by Class Associations and/or RYA.

## Format

Intensive coaching in small groups at home or abroad concentrating on:
- Preparation and Planning
- Speed - using two boat tuning
- Tactics and strategy - employing post race analysis.

## Content

As for racing clinics but with greater emphasis on:
**PREPARATION** to include:
- Programme planning
- Budgeting and sponsorship
- Goal setting
- Peaking Theory
- Physical fitness
- Weight and Diet

**SPEED** Technical Analysis of:
- Hulls; shape and structure
- Foils
- Rig
- Crew

**RACE ANALYSIS** to improve:
- Tactics
- Strategy
- Starting
- Mental attitude

## *Taught by*

Experienced RYA Racing Coaches
National Racing Coaches

# TOPICS FOR RYA RACING CLINICS

PRACTICAL ————————————————➤ THEORETICAL

|  |  |  |  |  |
|---|---|---|---|---|
|  |  |  | | Boat |
| **BOATHANDLING** |  |  | **PREPARATION** | Self |
|  |  | Speed |  | Regatta |
| Upwind |  | **TUNING** Sails |  |  |
| Downwind | TECHNIQUE | Spars | **COMPASS USE** |  |
|  |  |  |  |  |
| **STARTING** |  | **TACTICS** | **METEOROLOGY** |  |
|  |  |  |  |  |
|  |  | **RACING RULES** |  |  |
|  |  |  |  |  |
|  |  | Protests |  |  |

# CLUB RACING COACH/RACING INSTRUCTOR TRAINING

Training in adult Level 4 racing courses and the Red and White Badge Racing courses of the Young Sailors Scheme is given by a Club Racing Coach. The aim of the Club Racing Coach course is to provide experienced dinghy racing helmsmen and crews with the techniques necessary to run successful introductory race training courses and to assist Racing Coaches. Candidates may or may not already be RYA Dinghy Instructors.

The Club Racing Coach is trained by an RYA Club Racing Coach Tutor or by an RYA National Racing Coach. If the candidate is already an RYA Dinghy Instructor, then he becomes an RYA Racing Instructor; if not, he becomes an RYA Club Racing Coach. The only difference between a Club Racing Coach and a Racing Instructor is that the latter is also a qualified Dinghy Instructor and so has been trained to teach sailing to beginners and improvers.

A Club Racing Coach is trained to teach racing techniques and skills as outlined in RYA booklets G4 and G11 to sailors who are beginning their racing careers. This is an important area of racing as the lessons learned - and the way they are learned - should encourage a novice racing sailor to wish to improve. It is important that techniques and attitudes to racing are learned correctly, as they may be difficult to "unlearn" at a later stage.

Possibly the most valuable part of introductory race courses is the improvement of individuals' boat handling skills. For a Club Racing Coach to be able to improve a student's sailing skills the most important single attribute is the ability to diagnose and rectify faults.

Experience has shown that this is impossible unless the Club Racing Coach has sufficient background at a suitable standard in dinghy racing himself. For this reason, the potential Club Racing Coach is expected to have a minimum of five seasons' racing experience and have a good grasp of all aspects of the sport.

He must also be capable of imparting his knowledge to others, hence the emphasis in the Club Racing Coach course on teaching techniques and course organisation. As with every other aspect of instruction, a sense of humour is undoubtedly a great asset.

Where possible, single-handed boats will be provided for the Club Racing Coach course. Where this is not possible, it is suggested that a potential Club Racing Coach undertakes the course in the class of boat in which he normally sails. Class uniformity is as much of an advantage on a Club Racing Coach course as on ordinary race training courses.

As most on-water coaching is run from club launches or rescue boats, it is vital that Club Racing Coaches and RYA Racing Coaches are competent in powerboat handling. It is recommended that anyone lacking experience follows a course leading to the RYA National Powerboat Certificate (see RYA booklet G20).

Club Racing Coaches are encouraged to develop their coaching skills by working with an RYA Racing Coach. Those candidates with suitable experience may be recommended for further training as Racing Coaches by their Class Association, Regional Race Training Co-ordinator or a National Racing Coach.

## *Course Preparation*

In order to run a well-organised, informative and entertaining course, please remember the following:

## *Ashore*

- Choose a venue that can offer good facilities for lecturing, changing, launching/recovery, sailing, rescue and accommodation;
- Advertise your course in plenty of time in order to ascertain numbers;
  On receipt of applications, send accurate details about the course, together with a programme;
- Order stocks of logbooks, certificates, badges etc from your Regional Race
- Training Co-ordinator;
  If possible, get other coaches and Club Racing Coaches involved to help you run the course;
  Always prepare lectures; use OHP's from the RYA resource pack or prepare your own OHP's and/or 35mm slides; if using outside specialist lecturers, confirm their attendance in good time and ascertain what AV aids they will need;

## *Afloat*

- Have at least six portable racing marks with ground tackle available;
- Always be safety conscious - insist on buoyancy aids being worn afloat at all times, by students, trainers and helpers. Check that those using powerboats wear killcords;
- Always make notes of both good and bad points about candidates in order to give a thorough debrief ashore; use waterproof notes or a personal tape recorder to record coaching points; consider the use of video for boat handling exercises and a stills camera for boat tuning;
- Follow-my-leader exercises before and after a session provide good group control, are popular with students and allow a close examination of boat handling ability;
- Occasionally form protest committees involving those on the course, with coaches and trainers ensuring that the protest is structured correctly.

Suggested programmes of courses run by Club Racing Coaches and Racing Coaches are given in the next section, together with race training exercises.

# RYA RACE TRAINING COURSE PROGRAMMES

These programmes show typical course formats:

## RYA LEVEL 4/RED RACING BADGE COURSE

| | | | | | | |
|---|---|---|---|---|---|---|
| Course intro. Area familiarisation Safety & programme | Lecture: Introduction to racing How to prepare - starting procedure and techniques. Afloat: practise Debrief | L | Lecture: boat handling techniques - tacking - gybing. Afloat: practice starts & boat handling Exercises No. 1, 14, 3, 11 & 13 | Debrief Discussion | Lecture: Visual signals (basics) |
| Lecture: Starting techniques | Afloat: starting practice Exercise No. 14 Racing Exercises No. 1, 2 & 3 Debrief | U | Afloat: Boat handling techniques. Exercises No. 5, 6 & 7 Race Exercises No. 1 & 2 | Debrief Discussion | Lecture: Basic Racing Rules |
| Lecture: Protest procedure. Rule 68 & appendix No. 6 | Afloat: Boat handling Exercises No. 1, 11, 12 & 13 Race Exercise No. 3 Debrief | N | Afloat: match racing Exercise No. 4 | Debrief Discussion | FREE |
| Lecture: Crewing & spinnaker handling | Afloat: Boat handling techniques with spinnaker Exercises No. 5, 11 & 13 Debrief | C | Afloat: team racing Exercises No. 1, 2 & 3 | Debrief Discussion | Lecture: Basic Race Strategy |
| Lecture: Basic boat tuning | Afloat: Boat tuning in pairs Debrief | H | Afloat: Racing Exercise No. 1 or 2 | Debrief Discussion | Departure |

## RYA WHITE RACING BADGE COURSE

| | | | | | | |
|---|---|---|---|---|---|---|
| Course Intro. Area familiarisation Briefing | Afloat: Individual racing Exercise No. 1, 2 & 3 Debrief - discussion | L | Afloat: Boat handling Exercises No. 3, 5 & 11 Race Exercise No. 1 or 2 | Debrief Discussion | Lecture: Visual signals & meanings |
| Lecture:- Boat Handling techniques including spinnaker work | Afloat: Practise techniques Exercises No. 3, 5, 7, 11, 12, 13 Debrief - discussion | U | Afloat: Starting practice & techniques Exercises No. 14 & 19 Race Exercises No. 3 | Debrief Discussion | Lecture: Starting & techniques |
| Lecture:- Tactics | Afloat: Match racing Exercise No. 4 Debrief - discussion | N | Afloat: Team racing 2 v 2 Exercises No. 1, 2 or 4 | Debrief Discussion | Lecture: Racing Rules |
| Lecture:- Boat tuning | Afloat: Boat tuning - pairs or groups Race Exercise No. 1 or 2 Debrief - discussion | C | Afloat: Team racing 2 v 2 3 v 3 Exercise No 4 Starting practice - gate starts Exercise No. 20 | Debrief Discussion | Lecture: Racing Rules |
| Lecture:- Protests & procedure | Afloat: As required by trainer/ coach | H | Afloat: Individual racing Exercise No. 1 (large course) or 2 | Debrief Discussion | Departure |

# RYA BLUE RACING BADGE COURSE

| | | | | | |
|---|---|---|---|---|---|
| Course intro.<br>Discussion<br>Briefing | Afloat: Racing Exercises No. 1 & 2<br>Boat handling Exercise No. 11<br>Debrief - Discussion | L | Afloat: Boat handling Exercises No. 5, 10, 11<br>Race Exercise No. 3 | Debrief<br><br>Discussion | Lecture:<br>Physical fitness & training |
| 0700-0730<br>P.T.<br>Breakfast | Lecture: Championship preparation<br>Afloat: Boat handling Exercises 11, 12, 13<br>Race Exercise No 2<br>Debrief | U | Afloat: Match racing<br>Team racing 2 v 2<br>Exercise No. 4 | Debrief<br><br>Discussion | Lecture:<br>Racing Rules Definitions & parts 4 x 6 |
| 0700-0730<br>P.T.<br>Breakfast | Lecture: Starting & techniques<br>Afloat: Starting practice<br>Gate starts<br>Exercises No. 21, 22<br>Debrief | N | Afloat: Tactical Exercises No. 8 & 9<br>Racing Exercise No. 2 | Debrief<br><br>Discussion | Lecture:<br>Tactics |
| 0700-0730<br>P.T.<br>Breakfast | Lecture: Boat tuning<br>Sails & spars<br>Afloat: Boat tuning pairs & groups<br>Race Exercise No. 1 or 2 | C | Afloat: Boat handling Exercises No. 11, 12, 13, 16 & 18<br>Race Exercise No. 3 | Debrief<br><br>Discussion | Lecture:<br>Compass work |
| 0700-0730<br>P.T.<br>Breakfast | Lecture: Protests & procedures<br>Afloat: As required by coach | H | Afloat: Race Large course<br>Exercise No. 1 or 2 | Debrief<br><br>Discussion | Departure |

## RYA RACING CLINIC (CLASS ASSOCIATIONS)

| | | | | |
|---|---|---|---|---|
| Course Intro.<br>Discuss<br>Objectives | Briefing<br>Afloat: Short Race Exercise No. 1<br>Boat Handling Exercises eg: 3 & 12<br>Debrief | L<br><br><br>U | Briefing<br>Afloat: Technique Exercises eg: 7, 11 & 21<br>Short Race<br>Exercises No. 1 or 2<br>Debrief | Lecture/Discussion<br>eg: Preparation<br>Rigs<br>Meteorology |
| | Briefing<br>Afloat: Starting & tactical Exercises eg: 9, 14, 19, 20<br>Debrief | N<br><br>C<br><br><br>H | Briefing<br>Afloat: Boat speed Exercise No. 22<br>Race Exercise No. 1, 2 or 3<br>Debrief<br>Discussion<br>Depart | |

# RACE TRAINING EXERCISES

## Visual signals

Flags are not normally used, either simple number boards or three sail battens bolted together at one end are used for 3, 2, 1 minute starting signal accompanied by a sound signal. Flag signals should be used occasionally for familiarisation.

## Audible signals

Use either an effective whistle or horn. The following signals are used for boat handling exercises:

| | |
|---|---|
| 1 short blast: | Turn 90 degrees to starboard |
| 2 short blasts: | Turn 90 degrees to port |
| 1 long blast: | Hoist spinnaker - followed by |
| 1 long blast: | Lower spinnaker |
| Series of short blasts: | Stop or look out for hazard and keep clear |

The above signals are useful for exercises 11, 12 and 13.

### 1 Triangle Sausage/Sausage Triangle Course

- Used to evaluate standard at the beginning and throughout the race training programme
- Distances and angles between marks at Coach's discretion - normally short for boat handling, tactics and racing rules
- Additional rounds can be added.

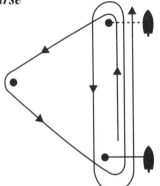

### 2 Olympic Trapeziod Courses

- Used to evaluate standard at the beginning and throughout the race training programme
- Distances and angles between marks at Coach's discretion - normally short for boat handling, tactics and racing rules
- Additional rounds can be added.

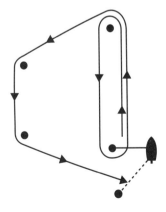

### 3 E Type Course

- For gybing, practising starts and tactics
- Distance between gybe marks depends on size of boat, wind strength, single or double handers, with or without spinnakers
- The distance should be enough to gybe and settle down before thinking about gybing again and also to establish maximum boat speed.

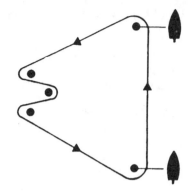

### 4 Sausage Course

- Used for both match and team racing
- Boats sailed in pairs with last boat causing the pair to lose
- Good for tactics, boat handling and racing rules
- Distance between marks again short, at Coach's discretion
- Boats must pass through line on the running leg
- Number of rounds at Coach's discretion.

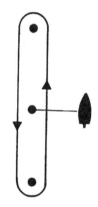

### 5 Box Course

- For boat handling practice, not a race
- Boats follow each other on the windward leg and five gybes on the run
- The Coach is anchored in the middle and if he wishes to talk to any of the squad, calls them alongside after they have rounded the bottom left hand mark
- He can feed them in again around the bottom right hand mark
- Also good for mark rounding practice.

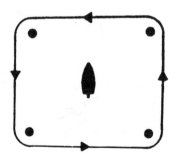

## 6 *Circular Course*
- For a small group of boats
- Roll tacking and gybing around the coach boat following closely behind each other
- The Coach can look closely at boat handling ability and comment on the spot.

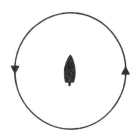

## 7 *Reaching Exercise*
- With or without spinnakers
- Tacking and gybing around the wing marks
- Coach can patrol the line to windward or to leeward looking at boat handling, trim, balance and sail trim.

## 8 *Triangle Exercise*
- Good for: starting, tactics, boat handling, boat speed and racing rules
- The Coach is to windward
- As the boat reaches the edge of the permitted lay-line, a whistle is blown and boats have to tack immediately to 'inside the triangle' or are disqualified
- No boat can call for water to tack under Rule 43.1, but must gybe around and pass under the stern of any boat on its weather quarter
- The boat which arrives at the Coach's boat first, rounds it (as the windward mark) and returns to the starting area.

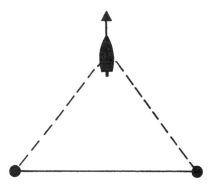

## 9 Leeward Mark Rounding Practice

- The only running start rounding a leeward mark and finishing on the same line
- This is a race to observe leeward mark roundings and the observance of Rule 42 as well as tactics, slowing down etc.

## 10 Slalom Exercise

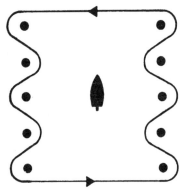

- Boat handling, tacking and gybing practice either a single line or as a double row for more boats
- Reaching across the top and bottom
- With a double row the Coach can be anchored in the middle as in Exercise 4.

## 11 Follow The Leader

- Boat handling on all points of sail, one behind the other as close as possible
- Speeds up reactions and helps people understand the characteristics of their boats
- Legs over the side to slow down is illegal!
- How do they slow down on a run? Pull the mainsail in and trim the boat aft to create more drag
- If any boat falls out of line they tack or gybe round and go to the back.

## 12 Tacking Exercise

- With a small group of boats tacking on the whistle
- Those whose boat handling is better start creeping out in front
- Re-group and start again.

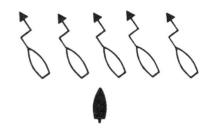

## 13 Gybing Exercise

As for Exercise 12 (with or without spinnakers).

## 14 Starting Exercise

- Short windward leg altering the line bias for each start
- This exercise can also be used for boat tuning runs if you wish to limit the area with a windward and leeward mark, ideally approximately 1 mile apart
- Two marks can also be set to leeward of the line to form a box in which boats must stay during the preparation period, to reduce their freedom (as it would be at any major event).

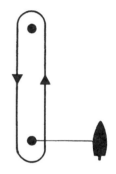

## 15 Reaching Exercise

- As for Exercise 7 but gybing around the wing marks (with or without spinnakers).

## 16 Boat Handling Exercise

- For both windward and spinnaker work, also for single handers
- This exercise can be used as a race in either direction or as a follow the leader exercise.

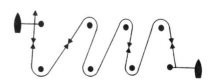

## 17 Speed Exercises

- To the mark and back, Olympic course, marks to port and starboard
- Sausage course for team or match racing, circular course for boat handling
- Can be used for various aspects of the sport.

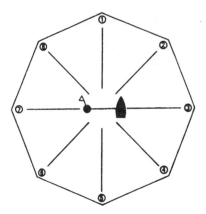

## 18 'X' Course

- Sailing through the line on each leg
- A boat handling exercise in a follow the leader situation or race.

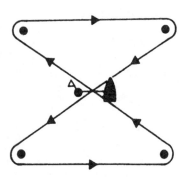

## 19 Starting Exercise For Beginners

- Must stay in starting box until preparatory signal to start
- If outside 'Sin Bin' watch a start.

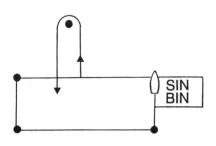

## 20 Beating Exercise

- Start between two boats
- Stay between them up the beat as they close each other approaching lay lines.

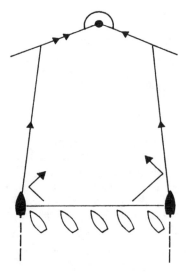

## 21 Acceleration Drill

- Boats position themselves on the imaginary start line between two free floating coach boats
- On audible signal they accelerate to full speed then stop and repeat.

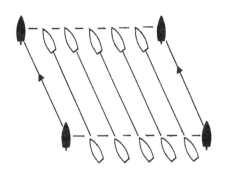

## 22 Two Boat Tuning

During a race training programme, boat tuning takes place during the latter part of a training session by which time the Coach can send people for boat tuning runs when both individuals and equipment are compatible. To achieve the best results from this exercise and to learn about rigs in various wind and sea states the boat tuning runs should be carried out as follows:

**A** In pairs with the training area designated by the Coach. One boat is in the safe leeward position slightly ahead and one crew sets their rig as to what they think is correct for the conditions and sails the boat as fast as possible. They sail until it is obvious that either one boat is going faster and/or pointing higher, they then stop. The other crew is allowed to make alterations to boat tuning controls to try to improve performance This is repeated over approximately one mile (long port and starboard tacks). Both boats now run downwind on opposite tacks alongside each other back to the leeward area discussing what has been achieved and learned.

**B** Same again but reverse roles.

**C** Same again but crews change boats to get the feel for the other boat in comparison to their own and to look at their own rig 'from the outside'.

**D** Similar strategies should be used for evaluating reaching and running speed.

Coaches can follow these pairs and advise on rigs, and use polaroid cameras to show photos ashore at the debrief.

On completion of pair tuning, the same can be done in groups of four or six. The two wing boats make no alterations whilst the others may make any necessary adjustments.

# ADVANCED INSTRUCTOR TRAINING

The Advanced Instructor must be capable of sailing to a very high standard and must have the background knowledge, technical ability and physical sailing skills to be able to demonstrate any of the techniques and manoeuvres within the Level 5 syllabus.

## *TEACHING LEVEL 5 - PERFORMANCE SAILING*

### *Rigging*

You must be able to rig a variety of dinghies including single handers, trapeze boats, spinnaker boats both conventional and asymmetric.

You should be able to show a knowledge and understanding of each different type of rig and be confident in your demonstrations.

### *Rig Controls*

**Mast foot position**
- Dictated normally by class rules
- Affects rake.

**Spreader deflection**
- Moving the spreaders forward stiffens the mast
- Moving them aft makes the mast bend more easily
- A heavier crew would therefore have the spreaders deflected further forwards than a lighter crew.

**Spreader length**
- Affects the pre-bend of the mast
- The longer the spreaders, the greater the pre-bend in the mast when the rig tension is put on, and vice-versa.

**Mast gate position (Mast ram and pre-bend)**
- By pulling the mast ram on you can straighten the mast, thus giving the mainsail greater power
- By easing the ram and pulling the pre-bend on you can bend the mast at deck level, thus flattening the mainsail for either very light conditions or strong winds.

### *Tuning*

You are expected to have detailed knowledge of the Five Essentials and how to utilise them at an advanced level.

**Sail Setting**
- Know how to set up the sails for light, medium and strong winds
- Be able to demonstrate the sail setting by using kicker, cunningham, rig tension, mainsheet tension, clew outhaul, main halyard tension, jib fairlead position.

**Kicker**
- This controls the amount of twist in the mainsail and also the leach tension
- It can also be used to flatten the mainsail by bending the mast forward at gooseneck level.

## Cunningham
- This is used in stronger winds
- As the wind increases then the maximum draft moves further aft thus producing more weather helm
- By pulling the cunningham on you bring the draft forward, improving the balance of the boat
- The cunningham is also used to free the upper leach, de-powering the sail in stronger winds.

## Main halyard tension
- This controls the mainsail luff shape
- Generally it should be tensioned so that there are small horizontal creases coming away from the mast
- Very low tension in light winds, increasing as the breeze builds to a lot of tension in strong winds
- The cunningham and main halyard tension have a similar effect on the mainsail
- The main halyard is normally set for the prevailing conditions whilst the cunningham is adjusted afloat and mainly comes into play in stronger winds.

## Mainsheet tension
- Generally controls the amount of twist in the mainsail leech
- Greater amount of twist needed in light winds to keep the sail from stalling, so the mainsheet needs to be eased
- As the wind increases the mainsail needs to be sheeted harder to reduce the amount of twist and tighten the leech.

## Clew Outhaul
- Controls the lower third of the mainsail
- Upwind in very light or strong winds the outhaul is pulled out to the black band
- In medium winds it may be eased slightly
- Downwind it is eased to produce more power in the rig, except for strong winds when you need to de-power the sail, when it is pulled on tight again.

## Rig tension
- Altered by adjusting the amount of tension that you have on the wire of the jib luff
- This is achieved by either a purchase system in the boat or a Highfield Lever situated on the side of the mast
- Generally high rig tension is required to point high
- If the rig tension is reduced you will lose pointing ability but will increase the fullness in the jib, thus making it more powerful
- In dinghies this isn't really an issue but in small keelboats this can help in light winds or choppy conditions.

## Jib luff tension
- Determined by how tight the head (or tack) of the sail is lashed to the eye in the jib luff wire
- The rig tension should be set up as normal and then the jib luff should be tensioned so as to just remove any horizontal creases
- By increasing or decreasing the jib luff tension you can move the camber in the sail either forward (increasing tension), or backwards (decreasing tension) to achieve the sail shape that you require.

### Jib fairlead position
- Controls the airflow over the jib.
- Initially set up the fairlead position so that the tell tales on the jib luff all lift together. This is a good starting point for medium airs.
- In stronger winds and possibly in very light conditions move the fairleads aft to enable the top of the leech to open and to flatten the foot of the sail. This twists the sail off so that it matches the twist in the mainsail.

The following tables give a rough guide as to how the sail controls are set for various wind strengths. These are only approximations and can vary between different classes of boat.

### Upwind

|  | Light | Medium | Strong |
|---|---|---|---|
| Kicker | off | just on | on tight |
| Cunningham | off | off | on tight |
| Rig tension | tight | very tight | eased slightly |
| Mainsheet tension | eased | on tight | vang sheet |
| Clew outhaul | tight | eased slightly | on tight |
| Main halyard | slack | tighter | very tight |
| Jib fairlead position | central/aft | forward | aft |

### Downwind

|  | Light | Medium | Strong |
|---|---|---|---|
| Kicker | off | just on | on |
| Cunningham | off | off | on |
| Rig tension | tight | very tight | tight |
| Mainsheet tension | ———— adjust as necessary ———— | | |
| Clew outhaul | eased | eased | tight |
| Main halyard | slack | tighter | very tight |
| Jib fairlead position | ———— move forward if possible ———— | | |

## *Balance and trim*

At an advanced level the balance and trim of a boat should become second nature. With experience both helm and crew should be continually shifting their position so as to keep the boat sailing most efficiently. This is not only important whilst sailing in a straight line but also whilst tacking, gybing, mark rounding, spinnaker hoists and drops etc.

The following table gives a rough idea of correct positions in the boat:

|  |  | Light | Medium | Strong |
|---|---|---|---|---|
| Upwind | Trim | forward | forward/central | central |
|  | Balance | leeward | side deck/hiking | hiking hard |
| Downwind | Trim | forward | central/aft | aft |
|  | Balance | leeward | side deck | side deck/hiking |

Whether you are sailing a single hander, two man dinghy or keelboat, this table gives an outline of general weight distribution within the boat.

## *Course Made Good*

At an advanced level, sailing an efficient course is not only having the sails set correctly, centreboard in the correct position, boat trimmed and balanced correctly and pointing in the right direction. Although all of these are very important, there are other factors to be taken into account:

- Wind direction and speed
- Wind shifts (headers and lifts)
- Wind bends (around headlands)
- Calms and gusts
- Tides - flood or ebb, areas of stronger/weaker flow, back eddies
- Other boats - moored boats, other sailing/power boats, ferries
- Geography - sand banks, shallow areas, islands, breakwaters

An advanced sailor should be taking these other variables into consideration along with the Five Essentials.

### Centreboard

- The centreboard (pivots) or daggerboard (lifts straight up and down) position is probably the most straightforward of the Five Essentials
- Generally the board is completely down whilst sailing to windward and is slowly raised the further you sail off the wind, until it is all the way up when you are running

### There are a couple of variances to the general rule

- When running it is sometimes useful to leave about 1/4 down as this aids steering and stability.
- In strong winds when sailing to windward, pull the board up slightly. This reduces the heeling forces and also moves the CLR (Centre of Lateral Resistance) further aft and in doing so reduces weather helm.
- In fast asymmetric boats the board is normally left completely down on the downwind legs. This is due to the fact that these boats rarely sail below a beam reach and more often than not, on a close reach due to the boat's speed through the water keeping the apparent wind well forward.

### Land Drills

Land drills are as important at Level 5 as they are at Level 1. They should be used whenever necessary. Good examples of Level 5 land drills are:

- Spinnaker hoists and drops
- Spinnaker gybes
- Trapeze work
- Demonstrations of sail and rig controls

From a safety point of view you must be careful when running these land drills that students do not injure themselves either falling out of the boat or dropping off the trapeze on to hard concrete!

## *Sailing*

Level 5 instructors must be confident in their ability to coach their students whilst they themselves are either in a dinghy with the student or in a coach boat alongside. This means that the instructor must be adaptable and confident on the water:

- You must be able to confidently sail a variety of dinghies including those with a trapeze and spinnaker (conventional or asymmetric)
- You must be able to demonstrate all skills in the Level 5 syllabus, including those specific to certain boats
- You must be aware of the differences, especially downwind, between single handers, conventional spinnaker boats and asymmetric boats

We will now look at some of the basic manoeuvres and techniques involved in the Advanced Endorsement. These are: trapezing, mark rounding, spinnaker hoists, gybes and drops.

## *Trapezing (single trapeze)*

### Getting out on the trapeze
- Crew hooks on and slides out over the gunwale keeping his weight on the trapeze wire
- He bends his forward leg and pushes out, at the same time holding the jib sheet in his aft hand
- Once out, it is important that he has the balls of his feet on the gunwale as close together as possible (the beginner will need his feet further apart initially to aid balance)
- From this position it is easy enough to move your weight to balance the boat by bending your knees.
- On most trapeze systems it is also possible to adjust your height (important for effective trapezing)
- Generally you need to trapeze as near to horizontal as possible to be most effective as a righting moment
- However, in certain conditions it is more advantageous to trapeze higher, ie in light winds, on a three sail reach, or in choppy conditions.

### Tacking
- Helm eases the mainsail and/or luffs slowly
- Crew bends his legs and swings back into the boat and unhooks from trapeze
- Crew uncleats and releases jib as helm pushes tiller away and tacks
- Crew pulls new jib sheet in as he crosses the boat
- Crew hooks on new trapeze and pushes out (see above)

## *Mark Rounding (double hander)*

### Windward mark
- Helm or crew eases kicker just before reaching the mark
- Helm eases main as he bears away
- Crew eases jib and balances the boat
- Boat must be kept flat or even slightly heeled to windward to assist bearing away (in strong winds both helm and crew move aft to stop the boat nose-diving)

- Centreboard up
- Ease outhaul and cunningham (if used) and adjust kicker as necessary
- Hoist spinnaker

**Leeward mark**
- Before the mark, pull on outhaul, cunningham and kicker (partially)
- Drop Spinnaker
- Centreboard down
- Helm luffs up around the mark sheeting in as required
- Crew sheets jib in unison and balances the boat
- Settle down, set kicker, mainsheet and jib sheet.

## *Mark rounding (single hander)*

**Windward mark**
- Ease outhaul
- Ease cunningham
- Ease kicker
- Daggerboard up
- Bear away and sheet out
- Shorten toestrap

**Leeward mark**
- Lengthen toestrap
- Pull cunningham on
- Daggerboard down
- Luff up around mark and sheet in
- Pull outhaul on
- Pull kicker on

## *Spinnaker hoists*

**Conventional - Leeward hoist (or spinnaker chute hoist)**
- Crew puts pole on
- Helm hoists spinnaker and balances boat
- Crew takes the guy and cleats, then sits on windward side deck
- Helm sits to leeward
- Crew takes sheet and adjusts as necessary

**Conventional - Windward hoist**
- Crew gathers spinnaker up into a ball and checks that the spinnaker guy is free
- Crew throws the spinnaker forward and the helm hoists quickly
- Communication is very important, otherwise the spinnaker will end up under the bow of the boat
- Crew puts pole on whilst helm plays the guy and the sheet
- Crew takes the guy and sits to windward
- Helm sits to leeward
- Crew takes the sheet and adjusts as necessary

### Asymmetric - hoist
- Helm bears away until the boat is in the safe sector, ie broad reach
- Crew pulls pole out
- Helm adjusts pole alignment if necessary (RS400 etc)
- Crew hoists spinnaker
- Helm luffs as crew sheets in
- As the boat accelerates the helm bears away and the crew eases the sheet
- Communication paramount to keep the boat achieving maximum VMG (velocity made good) ie sailing as low as possible but not losing the increased apparent wind strength, which enables the boat to sail low.

## *Spinnaker gybing*

### Conventional
- As the helm bears away the crew releases the guy and pivots the spinnaker around to windward
- Helm gybes the mainsail
- Crew stands up and swaps the pole to the new side whist the helm balances the boat and plays both the guy and sheet
- Crew takes over the guy and sits on new windward side
- Helm sits to leeward
- Crew takes sheet and adjusts as necessary

### Asymmetric
- Choose a good place to gybe when the boat is travelling fast (on the face of a wave) and in clear water
- Helm bears away and gybes the main
- Whilst the helm is bearing away the crew initially sheets in to assist the spinnaker to slide through the slot in front of the jib, then releases the old sheet and pulls quickly on the new sheet
- Helm re-aligns the pole (RS400 etc)
- Helm will probably have to luff slightly to pick up the apparent wind and then bear away as the boat speed increases.
- Crew eases sheet as boat bears away

## *Spinnaker drop*

### Bag
- Crew hands sheet to helm to play whilst pole is being removed
- Crew takes the pole off the mast and then off the spinnaker clew and then stores it
- Helm releases spinnaker halyard and crew pulls the spinnaker down, working up the leech first and then along the foot (this reduces the chance of the spinnaker twisting on the next hoist)
- Meanwhile the helm is looking ahead ready for the mark rounding

### Asymmetric
- Crew hands sheet to helm to play (this enables the spinnaker to be kept flying for longer, keeps the boat moving faster and keeps the spinnaker out of the water during the drop)

- Crew pulls in excess retrieval line (to stop spinnaker going under the bow and to speed up the drop)
- Crew uncleats pole outhaul and halyard and pulls spinnaker down by retrieval line
- As this is happening, the helm releases the pole alignment controls (if applicable), balances the boat and looks ahead ready for the mark rounding.

# TEACHING LEVEL 5 - SEAMANSHIP SKILLS

## Rudderless sailing
- Raise centreboard to 3/4 down
- Jib in, main out to bear away
- Main in to luff up
- Boats usually have slight weather helm when both sails filling
- Keep weight forward
- Heel to windward to bear away
- Heel to leeward to luff up
- Slow movements across the boat
- Can be easier if jib sheets tied together and mainsheet reeved as a simple purchase
- Following gybe keep jib to windward until settled on new course to prevent spinning

## Navigation
- Dinghy navigation is really pilotage
- You cannot do detailed chartwork in a dinghy
- Pre-planning is essential

## Charts
- Chart datum
- Measuring distances from latitude scale
- Soundings
- Drying heights
- Heights above mean high water springs
- Conspicuous features, lighthouses, headlands etc
- Common hazards, rocks, wrecks, overfalls etc

## Compass
- Compass rose
- Variation - corrections
- Awareness of deviation

## Tide tables
- High and low water
- Correction for BST
- Springs and neaps
- Rule of twelfths

## Tidal Stream Atlas
- Springs and neaps
- Interpolation by eye (do not attempt accurate interpolation)
- Marking up times of chartlets in Atlas
- Back eddies, affect of shallow water, overfalls

## Position fixing
- Principles of three point fix. Cocked hat
- Identifying transits - confirmation by hand bearing compass
- GPS - waypoints

## Buoyage
- Lateral marks - port and starboard
- Cardinal marks - north, south, east and west
- Special marks - yellow
- Safe water and isolated danger marks

## Use of hand bearing compass
- Pre-plan objects to be used
- Keep away from ferrous metal
- Allow card to settle
- Keep horizontal
- Keep top part of your body free to counter motion of boat
- Try to use bearings of 30 degrees or more apart
- Take bearing on the beam last (it changes quickest)
- Fixed objects are better than buoys

## Steering to a mounted compass
- If off course push tiller towards the number you want
- Make small tiller movements
- Try to head towards distant object - land or cloud temporarily, and check compass regularly
- Be honest to navigator about course actually steered

## Planning checklist
- Probable destination - approximate distances
- Viable alternative - approximate distances
- Weather forecast
- Times of high water at standard port
- Tidal gates on passage
- Times of favourable and adverse tides
- Critical heights and times of tide to cross bars etc
- Dangers en route, clearing lines, safe distance off etc
- Approximate course

- Food and drink
- Suitable clothing
- Harbour regulations
- Avoiding shipping
- Where to moor or beach at destination

## *Pilotage*

If you know where you are, with a chart and compass you should be able to identify where to go next.

- Courses and distances on chart
- Sail on transits to avoid being set sideways by tide
- At known positions eg buoys, confirm position or alter course
- Use laminated charts and chinagraph pencil
- Use Portland Plotter or equivalent (saves calculating correction for variation)

## *Emergencies*

- Pin point red flares
- Orange smoke flares

## *Meteorology*

### Sources of weather information

- Television
- Radio - shipping forecast, local forecast (details in nautical almanac)
- Weather fax
- Newspapers
- Coastguard
- Harbour master

### Terms used in shipping forecasts

- Beaufort scale
- Backing and veering
- Good, moderate and poor visibility

### Weather patterns

- Rapid barometric change usually indicates strong winds
- Anticlockwise wind circulation around lows
- Clockwise wind circulation around highs
- Warm front - lowering cloud, decreasing visibility, drizzle, south west winds
- Cold front - veer, cooler, north west wind, clear, showery
- Sea breeze - air over warm land rises, cool sea, air drawn ashore
- Fog - advection: warm air over cool sea, or radiation: land cools

### Observation afloat

- Squalls
- Gusts
- Approach of low pressure - cirrus clouds, hazy sun

# KEELBOAT INSTRUCTOR TRAINING

## Who can teach the National Sailing Scheme in keelboats?

A Senior Instructor with a Day Skipper practical certificate or higher, Yachtmaster Instructor

Dinghy Instructor with a two-day conversion course. All others: five-day Keelboat Instructor course.

Generally, the Principal of a Centre teaching in keelboats will be a Senior Instructor with a Keelboat Instructor endorsement, or a Yachtmaster Instructor.

Level 5 in keelboats should be run by an Advanced Dinghy Instructor with a Keelboat endorsement.

## Instructing in keelboats

The 'method' progression of learning to sail can be successfully taught in keelboats with a few simple modifications. Land drills are inappropriate, but the use of the boat controls for tacking and gybing can be demonstrated on a mooring.

The main differences from teaching in a dinghy are:

- The instructor will probably be teaching on board rather than in a rescue boat
- Allow students to take control if they are competent and avoid standing over them at the backstay
- There are only four essentials
- Techniques for grounding recovery
- Use of engine
- Man overboard technique
- Use of harnesses

With up to five students on board there is less helming time per person, although the crewing tasks are more involved. Move everyone around regularly. Little and often is appropriate for boat handling. For example the group can practise picking up moorings by approaching on the correct point of sail without actually securing to the buoy. This allows you to teach the principles and gives everyone a try quickly, allowing for slight misjudgements.

## Man overboard

Small keelboats can use the dinghy method but for larger boats (where a man held in the water will not effect the drift of the boat) use one or both of the following:

**Quick stop with engine:**

- Man overboard
- Pointer allocated
- Immediate heave to
- Drop lifebelt and danbuoy
- Start engine, check no ropes overboard
- Drop jib in hove to position
- Motor sail downwind until windex points at man
- Motor upwind
- Retrieve man at shrouds keeping propeller clear

### Reach-tack-reach man overboard
- Pointer allocated
- Immediate heave to
- Drop lifebelt and danbuoy
- Sail away 15 boat lengths on apparent beam reach
- Tack - can drop jib
- Point boat at MOB
- Ensure main can flap, if not dip downwind
- Spill and fill main on close reach aiming slightly upwind
- Retrieve MOB on leeward side

### Retrieval of MOB
With larger keelboats you need to have a method of retrieving people from the water. If they are conscious and not hypothermic use a ladder or foothold, eg bowline. Otherwise consider:
- Boarding ladder
- Detached mainsheet
- Handy Billy from boom or halyard
- Parbuckling with small sail
- Dinghy
- Helicopter harness or equivalent

## *Handling under power*
- At Level 2 keep the power manoeuvres to simple alongsides and moorings
- Demonstrate prop wash effect by engaging astern while secured alongside
- Practise turning boat under power
- Prepare for alongside - observe wind and tide, fenders and warps, position crew, communication, boat control, secure, use of springs

## *Moorings*
- Wind and tide
- Preparation (boat hook/warp)
- Communication
- Boat control

# *LEVEL 3 KEELBOAT*

## *Grounding*
- Leeshore dangers
- Awareness of state of tide
  If grounding on windward side:
- Ease or drop main, back jib, heel
  If grounding on lee shore:
- If quick you may be able to sheet in main and tack off
- If not, drop main quickly to avoid being blown on further
- If you have an engine heel boat and motor off
- With no engine, put out kedge
- If the tide is falling and no help is available, protect side of boat as it dries

## Emergency steering

Keelboats can be steered rudderless by lashing the helm exactly amidships and using sail trim and, to some extent, balance as in a dinghy. Emergency steering can involve the use of an oar, a spinnaker pole or boathook, or even a bucket attached to each quarter.

## Coastal passages

One day of a coastal Level 3 and Level 5 course is usually spent undertaking a day passage. Your planning must be first class. The Senior Instructor or Keelboat Instructor is responsible for the safety of the whole group and should not hesitate to change or abandon the plan if weather or other circumstances dictate.

When planning a trip consider the following:
- Weather
- Distance
- Student preparation - laminated chartlets, notebook
- Tides, streams, tidal gates, heights for entering and leaving harbours or anchorages
- Extra clothing, drink, food
- Extra equipment, tow lines, flares
- Radio contact, shore contact
- Emergency plan, refuge port
- Danger on route, shipping etc
- Landmarks on route, buoys etc
- Moorings, pontoon, anchorage at destination

The problem is to give everyone an experience of navigation rather than following the boat in front. Try to encourage everyone to become involved in the navigation but avoid splitting the fleet unless there is an instructor in each boat.

# MULTIHULL INSTRUCTOR TRAINING

Certain RYA Coach/Assessors are authorised by the National Coach to run specialist multihull instructor courses, which are open to candidates with the appropriate standard of multihull sailing ability. This is confirmed by a practical test identical to the pre-entry assessment outlined on page 35 with the exception that the rudderless sailing is omitted.

The instructor course itself has a similar format to that for dinghy instructors, with the exception that many of the boat handling techniques are different. Candidates are assessed by a specialist Coach/Assessor and if successful, are qualified as RYA Multihull Instructors.

Existing RYA Dinghy Instructors with the relevant multihull experience, who wish to gain a Multihull endorsement to their instructor certificate may do so by direct assessment. This assessment will include the pre-entry test outlined above and an assessment of practical multihull teaching techniques.

As the Dart 16 is the multihull class most widely used by RYA recognised teaching establishments, the notes which follow are aimed particularly at that class. Instructors teaching in other classes may wish to modify the techniques as appropriate.

## OUTLINE TEACHING METHOD/NOTES FOR MULTIHULLS

### Clothing/gear collection
- As for monohulls.

### Rigging/Launching
- Show students where to sit
- Demonstrate which items may be used as handholds, and which must not be used
- Hoist mainsail first
- Boat must be head to wind to hook on halyard lock
- Tack downhaul must not be tensioned yet, nor mainsheet attached
- Hoist jib and reeve jibsheets
- Attach rudders and lock up
- Lift bow and slide trolley under
- Show students how to hold onto the boat, with one hand on the forestay bridle, the other holding the bow
- Trolley boat into water and float off
- Stow trolley ashore
- Warn students of danger of placing feet under hulls in shallow water
- Crew holds boat head to wind as outlined above
- Helmsman attaches mainsheet
- Leave windward shore by sailing backwards; crew on each hull between bridle and main beam to lift sterns clear
- Control rate and direction of sternway by backing jib
- Leave other shores by sailing off gently, lowering windward rudder first
- When in clear water, stop to lower leeward rudder and tension tack downhaul

## Coming ashore
- Lift the leeward rudder first
- Ease mainsail tack downhaul
- Sail in slowly with the traveller eased off
- Crew sits on main beam and chooses right moment to slide off into the water on windward side to hold boat
- Meanwhile, helmsman lifts windward rudder when close to shore
- With an onshore wind the crew can dangle his legs in the water on the windward side, forward of the shroud to slow the boat down
- In strong winds with restricted access, boat is sailed in under jib alone

Coming ashore on sandy beaches with an onshore wind and large waves, the technique is different:

- Depower the mainsail
- Pick the right area and both helmsman and crew sit aft to keep the bows up
- At the right moment the helmsman trips the rudders and keeps going straight for the shore
- Take care when alighting from the boat and turning it head to wind
- Basic instruction from pebble beaches is not recommended

## Familiarisation/Joyride
- As for monohulls
- You should ensure that the trampoline is tight to give a greater feeling of security
- In light winds it is possible to have a 2:1 student:instructor ratio but above Force 3 the ratio should be 1:1 to avoid putting undue loads on the rig

## Orientation/Basic boat controls
Orientation is as for monohulls, but there are important differences in the basic boat controls session:
- Point out that multihulls do have brakes - the rudders
- The mainsail/jib controls used for monohull teaching are ineffective for multihulls
- Introduce two traveller positions: upwind/reaching and downwind
- The centreboard demonstration is generally inappropriate

## Going about
The teaching of successful tacking relies on two essential and related teaching points - maintaining sufficient boatspeed and sailing an efficient course to windward prior to tacking ie neither pinching nor close-reaching. It follows that it is not practical to tack from reach to reach so the existence of the No-Go-Zone must be introduced earlier than in monohull teaching.

The use of colour coded sheets and traveller can be a considerable advantage for beginners to avoid confusion. The tacking drill below includes the use of trapeze although this might not be appropriate for the very early stages of instruction. Having said that, it is essential that proper boatspeed and course are maintained into the tack.

**The basic manoeuvre is:**
- Helmsman checks inside and around boat, especially area into which he is going to sail, says 'ready about'
- Crew comes in off trapeze (if used) and unhooks harness and shouts 'Ready'
- Helmsman pushes tiller extension slowly and firmly until the tillers are at about 45 degrees to their normal position and holds tiller extension in that position
- Crew and helmsman both wait until the jib starts to cross the boat
- Helmsman then moves to a kneeling position on the centreline of the boat, facing aft
- He eases the mainsheet by about 15cm and clears the sheet
- Crew eases jibsheet and moves to centreline.
- Helmsman passes the tiller extension behind the mainsheet and crosses to the new windward side, picking up the mainsheet and uncleating it
- As the battens 'crack', helmsman takes up his new position, centres the tillers and trims the mainsheet. (In light winds, the helmsman needs to assist the sail to take up its new shape.)
- Crew then balances the boat as appropriate and trims the jib.

**The main teaching points about tacking a multihull are:**
- The time it takes
- Avoiding the temptation to slow down or pinch immediately before tacking.
- This might mean the crew staying out on the trapeze until the helmsman initiates the tack
- Overcoming the tendency to centralise the tillers too early
- Ensuring that the student does not let go of the extension
- The importance of trimming the mainsheet both before and during the tack. This means keeping the power on before starting a tack but remembering to ease the sheet as outlined above. In light winds, it will be impossible for the helmsman to reverse the mainsail camber when tacking by snatching the mainsheet falls unless he has eased the sheet prior to tacking.

**Going about practice/sailing to windward**
- As for monohulls, except that it is not practical to tack from reach to reach.

**The five essentials:**
1 **Sail setting** - the use of telltales nearest the head of each sail is introduced earlier than in monohull teaching, because of the fully battened mainsail. Introduce the use of the streamer on the forestay bridle as an aid downwind (the streamer should be at 90 degrees to the boat for optimum downwind sailing).
2. **Balance** - stress the different helmsman/crew positions for light and medium winds.
3. **Trim** - check that the boat is level by comparing waterlines forward and aft.
4. **Centreboard** - inappropriate for Darts. Other multihulls may have centreboards used in the same way as in monohulls. Downwind tacking may require small amounts of centreboard for steerage.
5. **Course sailed** - as for monohulls but emphasise the amount of time lost through inefficient tacking. Also stress the importance of tacking downwind.

## Downwind sailing/gybing

**The basic manoeuvre is**

- Helmsman sails on optimum downwind course (streamer at 90 degrees to boat) and checks around him, particularly the area into which he is going to turn
- Calls 'stand by to gybe'
- Crew checks area, replies 'ready' and moves to centreline of boat, picking up new jibsheet.
- Helmsman says 'gybe oh', pulling tiller extension steadily towards him until tillers are at 45 degrees to centreline. He moves to a kneeling position facing aft, close to the centreline
- Crew kneels on centreline, crouching low and facing forward (possibly holding onto toestraps)
- Helmsman lifts tiller extension and swings it abaft mainsheet falls, pulling the falls towards him with it
- Helmsman changes hands on tiller extension by passing forward hand forward of falls and grasping extension with it
- Aft hand is used to brake speed of gybe by catching falls of mainsheet. The inertia of that movement is used to swing the body to face the old sitting position
- Crew stays in position, keeping low
- Helmsman resumes normal position for new course
- Crew resumes correct position for prevailing wind and next course

**The main teaching points about gybing a multihull are**

- Students should not try to centralise the tiller in the middle of the gybe, as for monohull sailing
- Beginners should be discouraged from using the tiller bar, rather than the extension
- You must make students aware of the large area needed to gybe a multihull, particularly by beginners
- Ensure that slack mainsheet and traveller line are left on the centreline of the boat by the rear beam before gybing, to avoid kneeling on them and hence restricting their movement

## Further sessions

The ability to sail around a triangular course marks an important stage in basic instruction, as it shows that the student can tackle all points of sailing.

Teaching of man overboard recovery differs fundamentally from monohull teaching. Having regained control, the person left aboard will prefer to gybe rather than tack to get back to the man in the water, as it is quicker and the helmsman is in control throughout the manoeuvre. In addition, the man is recovered from between the hulls and if necessary over the main beam, rather than at the shroud.

## Capsize recovery drill

The golden rule about staying with the boat is more important with multihulls due to their high speed of drift when capsized in strong winds.

**The basic routine for recovery is**
- Helmsman and crew climb onto lower hull
- Crew moves forward to 'anchor' the bow in the water whilst helmsman moves aft to free the mainsheet and traveller line
- Helmsman moves forward again to grasp jibsheet or righting line
- Bow/mast allowed to swing into wind
- Crew leans out on sheet to right boat
- As it comes upright, helmsman grabs handles on bottom of trampoline to prevent a second capsize
- Helmsman and crew board via rear beam

**In the case of total inversion**
- Helmsman and crew move to transom and board there
- Helmsman ensures that mainsheet and traveller have been eased
- Crew retrieves jibsheet from windward side
- Both sit on leeward quarter to sink it and then start righting manoeuvre

The main teaching points are to encourage beginners to use the handholds and to emphasise that even with comparatively little righting moment, capsize recovery is possible.

## Teaching further skills

Once the basic techniques have been covered in RYA Level 1 and 2 courses, further multihull training follows the syllabi laid down in the RYA National Sailing Scheme Logbook G4, amended as appropriate with specialist techniques.

# SENIOR INSTRUCTOR TRAINING

The role of the RYA Senior Instructor is that of the sailing manager, the person responsible for organising sailing tuition at a teaching establishment according to RYA methods and standards.

The qualities required of a Senior Instructor are patience, resourcefulness, and the ability to deal with students and instructors. SIs should also have the organisational ability to ensure that courses are enjoyable, safe and informative.

Quite apart from his responsibility to his students, the Senior Instructor has a responsibility to his instructors, to his club or employer and the RYA.

Senior Instructor training is a combination of teaching and work experience. Courses are organised on a regional basis with minimum numbers in order to bring together candidates with a variety of backgrounds and instructing experience.

The specified course length is 40 hours, this may be split into two long weekends, with the separate sessions being run at different centres within a region. This gives candidates the opportunity of working at different places and hence being introduced to different operational problems.

As the SI course is likely to be the last formal course which most instructors attend, it aims to cover as many of their needs as possible, it is impossible to do this by didactic or dictatorial teaching. Instead, SI training and assessment consists of a mixture of discussion and task-related projects, together with short specialist inputs on specific subjects, either from Coaches running the course or from course members themselves.

Each practical session will be run by one of the course candidates and will form part of the continuous assessment of the course. The candidate will be expected to plan and organise the session, brief the other candidates, run the exercise and then debrief the group.

The Coach/Assessor will then debrief the whole group on the way the session was managed, so that every candidate will learn group control techniques by experience. In addition, the actual exercises used will be chosen to benefit the other course members who are participating in them. Such practical sessions could cover any part of the National Sailing Scheme and thus provide a good opportunity for candidates to refresh and improve their own skills.

## COURSE PLANNING

These parts of the SI course cover some topics which are relevant to all courses and others which are specific to certain levels. The general topics can be considered by following the framework of the 'Anatomy of a Club Course' devised by RYA Coach/Assessor Robin Cooter.

### Anatomy of the Club Course
1. Committee decision to run course, related to overall club programme. Decide costing
2. Confirm course with club committee regarding use of club facilities. Confirm liabilities and insurance

3. Advertise course. Distribute return booking forms or similar
4. Receive bookings, issue receipts/acknowledgements/acceptances
5. Plan theory programme, assess instructor and audio/visual input. Order RYA publications
6. Send out joining instructions
7. Send out letters asking for instructor help
8. Match available boats to instructors and students. Establish needs for extra boats and equipment
9. Make arrangements for teaching and safety boats and drivers
10. Arrange for Assessor if appropriate
11. Compile register and progress chart
12. Pre-course briefing for students
13. Start of course briefing for instructors
14. Consultation sessions with instructors
15. Debriefing at end of each session if possible
16. Formal conclusion of course (award of certificates)
17. Indication of students to follow-up
18. Thanks to instructors, helpers, club committee
19. Course evaluation - feedback from students and instructors
20. Final costing

## *Course Organisation*

The most important part of the Senior Instructor's role is day-to-day organisation of each course. Every course has four elements - the students, the instructors, the fleet/teaching facilities and the syllabus. It is the task of the Senior Instructor to ensure that they all fit together harmoniously. Apart from those caused by deteriorating weather conditions, problems usually arise from poor planning or a lack of communication between the SI, instructors and his students.

The SI is responsible for instructor/student ratios and matching. Be prepared to change crews or instructors if necessary, avoid the classic mis-matches of students, such as father/son or wife/husband. The SI is also responsible for group control ashore and afloat. Most teaching establishments have 'house rules' about gear stowage, how boats are to be left and slipway procedures. Ensure that all your instructors (including temporary staff ) know them.

Similarly, the SI is responsible for ensuring that all the students on a course are learning the right things at the right pace. One tactful way of ensuring, for example, that all your helpers follow the same techniques when teaching tacking and gybing is for the SI to give the first land drill demonstration.

Group control afloat is covered in some detail in the chapter on singlehanders on page 52, but in addition the SI is responsible for the provision of safety cover for the fleet. In many teaching establishments the distinction between teaching boats and safety boats is blurred, so you must ensure that each instructor realises the scope of his responsibilities.

In some cases and in some weather conditions the availability of safety cover will dictate or limit the scope of teaching, which in turn means that the SI is responsible for an alternative programme if the group cannot get afloat.

At the other extreme, the SI must try to continue effective teaching if there is too little wind, in extreme cases postponing part of the course to a later date. At all times, the SI must be able to recognise what is going on in the teaching fleet, either from a safety boat or from the shore, so that problems can be anticipated and avoided.

Before each practical session, the SI must be confident that each of his instructors has a clear idea of the aim of that session, so that they can confirm that the aims have been met during the debriefing.

It should already be clear that as an SI you have a great deal of responsibility, relying on your resourcefulness to solve problems which arise. Apart from directing the work of your instructors, you also have to assist and support them, particularly when they turn to you for advice. The following summary of brief questions might provoke further thoughts. How would you answer them?

## *Ten questions from instructors*

1. One of my students is learning far more quickly that the others. What do I do?
2. It's blowing Force 5 out there, What do I do? (day 2 of a beginners course)
3. What should I do with my hands when I'm lecturing?
4. You've asked me in to cover for Robin whilst he's away, how do I know what his students have covered so far? (third day of a Level 3 course)
5. How do I tell when my students are ready to move on to the next stage of the syllabus?
6. Bob and Sally say they're too old to take part in the capsize drill. What can I tell them?
7. What do I do if three of my Toppers capsize at once?
8. Why should I shave? (from a 22 year old male instructor)
9. Why should I bother with the kill cord on the outboard? It only gets in the way
10. How do I teach Jenny to sail? She's only got one hand.

You could be forgiven for thinking that some of those questions should never arise, but the fact is that your instructors will always look to you for advice. Even though they should know the answers, you must treat questions from instructors in just the same way that they should treat questions from students.

## *Catastrophe Clinic*

One of the advantages of a large Senior Instructor course is that it brings together candidates with a wide, varied collective experience of teaching sailing. One useful way of sharing that experience is by the exercise known as Catastrophe Clinic.

Each candidate writes a short outline of the worst things which have happened to them whilst teaching sailing. The outline should contain details of:

- The type of venue (inland, estuary, open sea)
- The size of fleet and type of boats
- The number of students and the level of course
- The number of instructors and teaching or rescue boats
- What happened

The group leader then collects all the examples and introduces them one by one for group discussion, with the author of each scenario remaining silent when his 'catastrophe' is discussed. After the group has discussed the problem and decided what they would have done in the circumstances, the author then explains what he actually did and why.

Some problems may result from the unexpected behaviour of instructors or students and will call upon the SI's resources of tact and diplomacy in finding a solution.

The real epics usually result from not one single problem but a string of circumstances, each one of which on its own might not have been so serious. The horror of multiple capsizes in deteriorating weather conditions, possibly with dangerous lee shore or commercial shipping nearby, calls for clear thinking to establish priorities and act decisively. The two Golden Rules in such circumstances are:-

- Count heads.
- Save people before property.

One recurring theme which is not highlighted above is that of the student with a health problem, either unknown or undisclosed. Examples range from the teenage diabetic on a residential course who forgets his medication in the excitement of the activity, to the middle aged man who suffers a suspected heart attack during a capsize recovery session and the woman who collapses in the hot shower after sailing, for reasons totally unconnected with the activity.

All have specific lessons for the Senior Instructor but the overall message is that the SI in control of the group must know of any health problems. The usual way of finding out is to require all students to complete a health declaration. A standard form is shown on page 7.

## *Session Planning Exercises*

In these exercises, shown in detail on the next page, assume you are the SI of a fleet at a centre, the centre owns; Optimists (12), Toppers (24), Wayfarers (8), Lasers (12) and 6 Jeanneau Safety Boats, there are also 3 RIBs and a 25' Diesel Launch. Other SIs will be working with their fleets so it is essential you use the minimum possible equipment. In each case you are given sufficient information to plan a day.

| No of students | Session required | No of instructors | Weather |
|---|---|---|---|
| 12 children | Day 1 of Stage 1 | 2 plus you | Summer, sunny and calm |
| 14 children | Day 1 of Stage 1 | 2 plus you | Autumn, wet and squally, SW 4 to 5 |
| 30 children | Day 3 of Stage 1 including day sail and picnic | 6 plus you | Summer, fair, E 2 to 3 |
| 27 children | Day 2 of Stage 3 | 5 plus you | Summer, fine and calm |
| 17 children | School group on second afternoon session during summer term | 4 plus you | Rain, WSW 7 |
| 15 pupils | Planning discussion with teacher from local Prep School. Wants 8 2-hour sessions | | |
| 21 children | Various abilities from stages 1 to 3 - don't know how many of each. Day 1 of a 5 day residential course | 3 plus you | Summer, fine, SW 2 |
| 15 children | 5 beginners, 2 hold Stage 1, 7 hold Stage 2, 1 holds Stage 3 | 2 plus you | Spring, fair, NNW 3 to 4 |
| 13 adolescents | Day 1 of Level 2 | 2 plus you | Summer, cloudy, showers, WSW 2 to 6! |
| Mixed ladies and teenagers, total of 11 | Unknown ability and arriving in one hour | 1 plus you | Spring, sunny, W1 to 2 |
| 18 Public School children aged 14 to 15 | At Level 3 standard | 2 plus you | Winter, sunny, W 5 to 6 |
| 37 mixed ability teenagers (13 to 17 years) | Day 4 of residential holiday | 6 plus you (you have been asked to stand in as SI) | Easter, sunny with showers, SW 3 to 4 |

| | | | |
|---|---|---|---|
| 2 families:<br>Family 1 - parents (32 and 34) with children (6 and 8)<br>Family 2 - parents (48 and 49) with children (14 and 15) | They want to sail together if possible and are thinking of buying a Wayfarer for cruising | 2 plus you | Easter, SW 4 |
| 6 children (6 to 8 years) | Birthday treat. The parent who booked them wants them to sail in a boat with an instructor so they will be safe | 1 plus you | Autumn, S 3 to 4 |
| 9 adults | Day 3 of Level 2. 3 clients do not want to do any exercises afloat as they don't want Level 2 - they want to sail to a nice pub for lunch. 4 clients want Level 2 so they can hire a boat. 3 are indifferent so long as they sail | 2 plus you | Summer, SW 3 |
| 6 physically challenged but mobile teenagers with 4 helpers | | 2 plus you | Summer, rain expected, E 4 |
| 35 Primary School children | 2 hour taster session | 11 plus you | Spring but you missed the forecast |
| 4 children with emotional and behavioural difficulties.<br>1 adult carer | Gentle taster sail. Adult carer is a dinghy Coach but you don't know her. Rumoured that children can be violent for no apparent reason | Assistant instructor plus you | Summer, SW 2 |

In some of these scenarios, you might encounter problems, for example, with safety cover. You know that the centre is busy and operating to its limit. There may be situations you haven't met before, discuss your concerns with the Training Coaches or your friends on the course and try for the best plan. Remember, if there is a situation you haven't met then your Instructors probably haven't met it either.

## *Session Planning Afloat*

**Assume a group of 8 students in each session unless otherwise stated**

**Task 1**

Devise a competitive game or activity to improve reaching and downwind sailing skills. You should be prepared to adapt to the prevalent conditions and use all the facilities available on the boats.

Group: Enthusiastic Level 3 Sixth formers.

Craft:   505, Laser Fun x 2, Laser 2 x 2, Lasers x 3, Wayfarer, Dory.

## Task 2

The group has asked you if they are ready to go on a level 5 course. Devise a session which demonstrates to you and them what is required and whether or not they are ready for the course.

Group: Potential Level 5 Adults.

Craft:   Lasers x 4, Picos x 4, Wayfarer, Launch

## Task 3

You have a group of paraplegic students who have come to your centre to do a 5-day Level 2 course. Each has an able bodied helper who also wants to sail. You also have an assistant instructor. Devise a session to give them their first session afloat.

Group: Physically Handicapped  and Able Bodied Association.

Craft:   Wayfarers x 4, Launch

## Task 4

Devise a fun session to get your students using a trapeze properly. They have already had a land drill and just need a quick reminder. Out of your seven students 2 are nervous and the rest have a 'go for it' attitude.

Group: Level 3 Adults.

Craft:   505 x 2, Laser 2 x 2, Wayfarer with trapeze, Laser Fun, Dory.

## Task  5

Your sailing establishment has applied to become RYA Recognised. An Inspector is going to visit and wishes to see a course of training in progress. Devise a practical programme lasting about 30 minutes which demonstrates the scope of your work.

Group: Level 3  teenagers.

Craft:   Laser x 4, Topper 2 , Pico x 2, Launch

## Task 6

Remind your group of the principles of planing. If conditions allow devise an exercise to practise and develop these skills. If wind is light devise a training exercise to improve light weather spinnaker skills. Liaise with centre and ensure your group assists in packing up all craft.

Group: Enthusiastic young adults.

Craft:   505, Laser Fun, Laser 2 x 2, Laser x 2, Dory

## Task 7

You are asked to run a training course in preparation for the instructor Pre-entry assessment. Using your instructors, have the three following activities running simultaneously: triangular course using all boat's facilities; rudderless sailing; tight circles. Move crews around.

Group: Level 5 Adults.

Craft:   505, Laser 2 x 2, Laser Fun, Launch.

## Task 8

Your group of level 2 candidates have completed their course and would like to learn more about racing. Devise a session to arouse their competitive instincts but involve more than sailing as fast as possible round buoys.

    Group:  Level 2 teenagers

    Craft:    Lasers x 4, Picos x 4, Launch or small Dory.

### Task 9

You wish to prove to a group of sceptical club sailors that attention to the five essentials really can improve boat speed. By contrasting the good with the bad demonstrate and try to convince them that attention to these details will help them move up the fleet.

    Group:  'bottom of the fleet' club sailors.

    Craft:  Lasers x 4, Picos x 4, Launch.

### Task 10

Devise and execute a fun session to improve awareness and boat handling skills for this enthusiastic group so that they can get maximum benefit from prevailing conditions and using all the facilities on the available craft. Liaise with centre to ensure all craft are left as they wish.

    Group:  Level 5 sixth formers.

    Craft:    505, Laser Fun, Laser 2 x 2, Dory.

## *Senior Instructor Assessment*

Throughout your SI Course you will be assessed on your ability to plan, organise and run practical sessions, and on your input to shorebased sessions. In particular, the course organiser is looking for:-

- Aims clearly stated (did the session have clear objectives?)
- Briefing was complete and clear (did the group know what was required?)
- Sailing area identified
- The leader could be clearly identified.
- The whole group was involved.
- Enthusiasm was maintained
- Problems were solved.
- Signals (two way) were established including 'Abandon'
- On-water coaching took place
- Group control was maintained (no unnecessary delays) ashore and afloat.
- The clients were carefully debriefed and problems discussed and solved.
- Session achieved all objectives.
- Clients' questions were answered
- Clients were informed of their successes
- The follow-on session was described
- The equipment was carefully put away after the session

## *Good relationships with others*

In addition, the course organiser will be applying an assessment based on his experience of the RYA Coaching Scheme to decide whether you meet the requirements of a Senior Instructor as defined on page 16. If he is unable to confirm that you have successfully completed the course, the Coach will outline the reasons for that decision and an action plan needed for future success.

# COACH/ASSESSOR TRAINING

## Training Instructors

Instructors teaching sailing follow the process of brief-task-debrief (page 21), with the task being a sailing skill. Instructor courses follow the same principle except that the task is teaching. The problem for the Coach/Assessor running an instructor course is organising teaching sessions which are as real as possible.

The trainee instructor can practise teaching to either a) the fellow trainees, b) the Coach/Assessor, or c) 'real' beginners. The presence of the Coach/Assessor is always going to affect the relationship between instructor and pupil but a skillful Coach/Assessor can minimise nervousness and the false nature of the situation. While 'real' students are a useful part of the instructor training course, these volunteers can only realistically be arranged for a limited number of sessions. Also, from the viewpoint of the beginners, the instruction can be rather disjointed and possibly delivered by an instructor who is far from expert.

## Debriefing instructors

When debriefing avoid having a conversation about sailing. The Coach/Assessor must concentrate on the delivery of the instruction. The section of this book on keeping students informed (page 23) is particularly relevant on instructor courses.

## Organising an instructor course

- Inform the Regional Coach and RYA HQ
- Ensure candidates are aware of the eligibility requirements including the pre-entry sailing test
- Arrange for a second Coach/Assessor on the final day. The course is five days and the moderation should be on the last day
- The teaching ratio is 6 trainee instructors to 1 Coach/Assessor, with a second Coach/Assessor on the final day

## The training course

Most Coach/Assessors running instructor courses spend about 2 days on the method and Level 1 and 2, a day in single-handers, a day on Level 3 teaching and a final moderation day drawing together all elements of the course.

## Assessing instructors

The instructor course is much harder to assess than a sailing course because good and bad teaching is dependent to some extent upon personality as well as presentation skills. Coach/Assessors can be faced by technically good sailors who, for example, have problems relating well to students, become aggressive or anxious or show other traits which make them unsuitable as instructors. Coach/Assessors are not qualified to assess personality and should take the view that instructors are doing their best to do well but might need assistance in teaching skills. If at the end of the course the Coach/Assessor has strong reservations about a trainee instructor's suitability to do the job, the debrief should be restricted to communication and teaching skills rather than a character assassination. The second Coach/Assessor is invaluable here and prevents a personality clash influencing the overall result.

Unsuccessful candidates should be given an action plan. If the problem is a poor rapport with students, it is safer to require a further training course with assessment by a further two Coach/Assessors.

A deferment based on a lack of knowledge of a straightforward skill such as the RYA method can be reassessed over a short period by one Coach/Assessor.

## *Moderation*

One of the difficulties of conducting a moderation is that the candidates are likely to be nervous and see the day as a stressful examination rather than an opportunity to demonstrate their teaching skills.

The moderator has to handle this situation carefully, mainly because a nervous candidate can produce the wrong result.

**To reduce tension**
- Start by giving a reasonably straightforward practical task to teach. If chosen well it should be successful. Say 'well done'. This makes the assessment seem achievable
- Be honest about the intentions of the day. Yes, it is an assessment but there are no tricks and the tasks are chosen to give maximum opportunity to show the skills learnt
- Have an open and honest approach to encourage the candidates to ask if unsure about a task
- Take an interest in the candidate

**Tension is increased by**
- Being secretive about the test and the tasks
- Lack of communication or prolonged periods of silence
- Self-importance of the Assessor
- Setting unrealistic scenarios
- Quick fire or irrelevant questioning
- Disparaging remarks

The moderator must discuss with the training Coach/Assessor how the day needs to be organised. The training Coach/Assessor can continue the course during the moderation day. Many Coach/Assessors prefer to 'go in cold' with no knowledge of the candidates, whilst others prefer to concentrate on marginal candidates. Either way, the final result must be given by both Coach/Assessors who have discussed each candidate and come to a result which will enhance the RYA training scheme.

# NATIONAL VOCATIONAL QUALIFICATIONS FOR DINGHY INSTRUCTORS

The RYA is accredited to train and assess for National Vocational Qualifications at Level 2 in both dinghy and windsurfing instruction. The NVQ Level 2 is roughly equivalent to the standard of the RYA Dinghy Instructor or Windsurfing Level 2 Instructor award. As well as covering the skills required of those courses, the NVQ assessment also covers other skills associated with working at a sailing centre such as contributing to the running of the centre, dealing with clients off the water as well as on, knowledge of health and safety issues etc. These skills are represented by 'units of competence' which make up the qualification:

Unit
D43   Prepare for coaching sessions
D44   Conduct coaching sessions
C35   Deal with accidents and emergencies
D13   Establish and maintain relationships which support the coaching process
B11   Support the development of the sport/activity

As this is a vocational qualification it must be assessed in the candidate's work place and so is most appropriate and easily achievable for instructors already working at a sailing centre, either on a full time or casual basis. There is no requirement for instructors to hold an NVQ but some employers, particularly local authorities, may prefer to employ instructors who hold or are working towards the award.

Anyone wishing to gain an NVQ must complete a portfolio of evidence showing that they have been doing the job of an instructor in a sailing centre with 'real' students, to a satisfactory standard. They will then be assessed and their portfolio will be reviewed to ensure that all areas of the award have been covered. The most common way for an instructor to work towards the NVQ is to complete the RYA instructor course first. The course and the skills learnt on it can then make a large contribution to the candidate's portfolio. It is possible for a candidate to achieve the NVQ without having done the instructor course first. However, it is likely that the process of gathering evidence and being assessed will take considerably longer.

If you would like further information on NVQs in dinghy sailing or windsurfing instruction, please contact the RYA.

# CHILD PROTECTION INFORMATION

Written in conjunction with the NSPCC

It is now widely accepted that it is the responsibility of every adult to protect children from abuse. All children have a right to be protected from all forms of abuse and discrimination and to be treated equally regardless of age, gender, racial origin, culture, religious belief, language, disability or sexual identity.

Child abuse, and particularly child sexual abuse, can arouse strong emotions in those facing such a situation and it is important to understand those feelings and not allow them to interfere with your professional judgement.

The sailing instructor, particularly if working in a centre where children attend on a regular, sessional basis, may become an important link in identifying a case where a child needs protection. Child abuse may come to light in a number of ways:

- A child may tell you what has happened to them
- From a third party (for example, another child)
- Through the child's behaviour
- A suspicious, unexplained injury to the child

These notes are intended to provide a guide to help you identify signs of possible abuse and know what action to take in such cases.

## *The main forms of abuse are*

### Physical abuse

This is where adults physically hurt or injure children. Hitting, shaking, squeezing, burning or biting are all forms of physical abuse. Giving children alcohol, inappropriate drugs or poison is classified as physical abuse. Attempted suffocation or drowning also comes within this category.

### Sexual abuse

Girls and boys are abused by adults who use children to meet their own sexual needs. This might be full sexual intercourse, masturbation, oral sex, anal intercourse, or fondling. Showing children pornographic magazines or videos is also a form of sexual abuse.

### Emotional abuse

Persistent lack of love and affection damages children emotionally. Being constantly shouted at, threatened or taunted can make the child very nervous and withdrawn.

### Neglect

This is where an adult fails to meet a child's basic needs, like food or warm clothing. Children might also be constantly left alone unsupervised. Sometimes adults fail to, or refuse to, give their children love and affection. This is emotional neglect.

Abuse in all its forms can affect a child of any age. The effects can be so damaging that they may follow an individual into adulthood.

## Identifying signs of possible abuse

Recognising abuse is not easy, even for individuals who have experience of working with child abuse. Most children will receive cuts, grazes and bruises from time to time and their behaviour may give reason for concern. There may well be other reasons for these factors other than abuse, but any concern should be immediately discussed with a senior colleague to assess the situation.

**Warning signs which may alert instructors to the possibility of abuse can include**

- Unexplained bruising, cuts or burns on the child, particularly if these are parts of the body not normally injured in accidents
- An injury which a parent or carer tries to hide, or for which they might have given different explanations
- Changes in behaviour such as the child suddenly becoming very quiet, tearful, withdrawn, aggressive, or displaying severe tantrums
- Loss of weight without a medical explanation
- An inappropriately dressed or ill-kept child who may also be dirty
- Sexually explicit behaviour, for instance playing games and showing awareness which is inappropriate for the child's age.
- Continual masturbation, aggressive and inappropriate sex play
- Running away from home, attempted suicides, self-inflicted injuries
- A lack of trust in adults, particularly those who would normally be close to the child
- Eating problems, including over-eating or loss of appetite

Remember, the above signs do not necessarily mean that a child has been abused. If you are concerned about the welfare of a child, however, you must act. Do not assume that someone else will help the child; they might not.

## Listening to the child

Remember that the child's welfare is paramount, and this must be the most important consideration.

Listen carefully to any complaint or allegation by the child, and tell and show the child that you are taking them seriously.

If a child's behaviour or your observations give rise to concern, then talk to the child sensitively to find out if there is anything worrying them.

Keep questions to a minimum, but make sure you are absolutely clear about what a child has said so that you can pass on this information to professionals who are trained and experienced in investigating possible child abuse.

Acknowledge how difficult and painful it must have been for them to confide in you and reassure the child, stressing that they are never to blame.

Stay calm; don't take hasty or inappropriate action.

Don't make promises which you may not be able to keep.

Don't take sole responsibility; consult a senior colleague so that together you can begin to protect the child, and also so that you can get some support for yourself in what could be a difficult situation.

As soon as possible after talking with the child, make a written record of what the child said, how they were behaving, and what you did in response.

## Talking to parents and carers

It is possible that a relationship with parents and carers will have been established and as a general principle it is important to be open and honest when dealing with them.

There may be circumstances, however, when it is not appropriate for parents to be informed immediately of the concerns you have, as this may prejudice any investigation and may place the child at even greater risk.

Always discuss your concerns first with a senior colleague; contact with parents could be delayed until you have sought advice from one of the professional agencies who have been notified (see below).

## Responding to child abuse; what to do if you are concerned

Remember that it is not your responsibility to decide if child abuse has occurred, but it is your responsibility to take action, however small your concern.

Inform a senior colleague who will take responsibility for seeking any additional advice and for contacting the local Social Services Department, the Police or the NSPCC, who are trained to deal with such situations and have the necessary legal power to protect the child.

If no senior colleagues are available, or concerns for the child remain, then you must contact the local Social Services Department, the Police or the NSPCC yourself. You do not have to give your name, although this will be helpful to the agency making enquiries into the matter and who may need to talk to you again.

The agency receiving your referral will take responsibility for ensuring that appropriate investigations are undertaken and the child protected.

## Allegations of abuse against members of staff

Child abuse can and does occur outside the family setting. Although it is a sensitive and difficult issue, child abuse has occurred within institutions and may occur in other settings. The following notes contain guidance on recruitment and what to do if there are concerns that a member of staff is abusing a child.

## Recruitment (paid staff and volunteers):
## Supervision and monitoring

All applicants for work, whether paid staff or volunteers, should be subject to scrutiny. Application forms should be designed to elicit information about the applicant's past career (requiring explanations for any gaps) and to establish any criminal record.

Although positive vetting is not specifically recommended, applicants should signify their consent to checks being made with police and social services and should provide references, preferably including at least one regarding previous work with children. References must always be taken up.

The Department of Health operates a consultancy service on an advisory basis whereby local authorities and voluntary agencies are able to check on the suitability of those proposing to work with children.

The Department of Education and Science also has a 'List 99' which contains information about people whom the Secretary of State for Education and Science has adjudged to be a risk if seeking subsequent employment which will involve contact with children. Further advice about these two systems can be obtained from your local Social Services Department and Education Department.

It is important for Principals to review the operation of their establishments to minimise the situations where any adult is left alone with a child (or group of very young children).

## *What to do if there are allegations of abuse against a member of staff*

Again, remember it is the child's welfare which must be of paramount importance.

Follow the guidelines in the section dealing with 'Listening to the Child'.

Refer the matter to a senior colleague so that the appropriate child protection procedures can be followed. The senior member of staff must inform the Social Services Department, the Police or the NSPCC.

If your concern is about a senior colleague, then seek advice from another senior member of staff who should ensure that the child protection procedures are implemented and the Social Services Department, the Police or the NSPCC are informed.

It is important to understand that a member of staff reporting a case of child abuse, particularly by a colleague, may undergo a very high degree of stress, including feelings of guilt for having reported the matter. It is therefore very important to ensure that appropriate counselling and support is available for staff in such a situation.

# NATIONAL COACHING SCHEME PERSONAL LOG

| DATE | TYPE OF BOAT | HOURS EXPERIENCE | | ACTIVITY AND WEATHER CONDITIONS | | AUTHORISATION |
|---|---|---|---|---|---|---|
| | | Senior Instructor or Coach | Instructor or Race Trainer | Level of Course or Training Programme | Max. Wind Speed | Establishment/ Principal |
| | | | | | | |
| | | | | | | |
| | | | | | | |
| | | | | | | |
| | | | | | | |
| | | | | | | |
| | | | | | | |
| | | | | | | |
| | | | | | | |
| | | | | | | |
| | | | | | | |
| | | | | | | |
| TOTALS C/F | | | | | | |

**TOTALS B/F**

| DATE | TYPE OF BOAT | HOURS EXPERIENCE | | ACTIVITY AND WEATHER CONDITIONS | | AUTHORISATION |
|---|---|---|---|---|---|---|
| | | Senior Instructor or Coach | Instructor or Race Trainer | Level of Course or Training Programme | Max. Wind Speed | Establishment/ Principal |
| | | | | | | |
| | | | | | | |
| | | | | | | |
| | | | | | | |
| | | | | | | |
| | | | | | | |
| | | | | | | |
| | | | | | | |
| | | | | | | |
| | | | | | | |
| | | | | | | |
| | | | | | | |
| | | | | | | |

**TOTALS C/F**

| | | TOTALS B/F | | | | |
|---|---|---|---|---|---|---|

| DATE | TYPE OF BOAT | HOURS EXPERIENCE | | ACTIVITY AND WEATHER CONDITIONS | | AUTHORISATION |
|---|---|---|---|---|---|---|
| | | Senior Instructor or Coach | Instructor or Race Trainer | Level of Course or Training Programme | Max. Wind Speed | Establishment/ Principal |
| | | | | | | |
| | | | | | | |
| | | | | | | |
| | | | | | | |
| | | | | | | |
| | | | | | | |
| | | | | | | |
| | | | | | | |
| | | | | | | |
| | | | | | | |
| | | | | | | |
| | | | | | | |
| | | | | | | |
| | TOTALS C/F | | | | | |

| | | TOTALS B/F | | | | |
|---|---|---|---|---|---|---|

| DATE | TYPE OF BOAT | HOURS EXPERIENCE | | ACTIVITY AND WEATHER CONDITIONS | | AUTHORISATION |
|---|---|---|---|---|---|---|
| | | Senior Instructor or Coach | Instructor or Race Trainer | Level of Course or Training Programme | Max. Wind Speed | Establishment/ Principal |
| | | | | | | |
| | | | | | | |
| | | | | | | |
| | | | | | | |
| | | | | | | |
| | | | | | | |
| | | | | | | |
| | | | | | | |
| | | | | | | |
| | | | | | | |
| | | | | | | |
| | | | | | | |
| | | | | | | |
| TOTALS C/F | | | | | | |

| | TOTALS B/F | | | | | |
|---|---|---|---|---|---|---|

| DATE | TYPE OF BOAT | HOURS EXPERIENCE | | ACTIVITY AND WEATHER CONDITIONS | | AUTHORISATION |
|---|---|---|---|---|---|---|
| | | Senior Instructor or Coach | Instructor or Race Trainer | Level of Course or Training Programme | Max. Wind Speed | Establishment/ Principal |
| | | | | | | |
| | | | | | | |
| | | | | | | |
| | | | | | | |
| | | | | | | |
| | | | | | | |
| | | | | | | |
| | | | | | | |
| | | | | | | |
| | | | | | | |
| | | | | | | |
| | | | | | | |
| | | | | | | |
| | TOTALS C/F | | | | | |

# RECOMMENDATIONS FOR COACHING COURSES

## *ASSISTANT INSTRUCTOR*

Training and assessment record

Principal's initials

The candidate:
Is aware of safety requirements                                              _____

Is aware of teaching sequence used when teaching beginners        _____

Is aware of the teaching points for each part of the sequence       _____

Is proficient in teaching shore drills                                          _____

Is proficient in teaching capsize recovery                                  _____

The candidate has demonstrated competence as an Assistant Instructor to the standards laid down by the RYA.

Signed (RYA Principal)

Name in capitals

Recognised teaching establishment

Date

*PLACE YOUR ASSISTANT INSTRUCTOR CERTIFICATE HERE*

# RYA DINGHY/KEELBOAT/INSTRUCTOR

## Eligibility
Minimum age 16
Valid first aid certificate
RYA Powerboat Level 2 certificate
Pre-entry sailing assessment completed within one year prior to the instructor training course

## Pre-entry Assessment Completed
Venue *MEHCEHAM RYTHG*    TIDAL/~~INLAND~~

*SC*

Date *21-9-02*

Type of boat:  DINGHY/~~KEELBOAT/MULTIHULL~~

Approved by (RYA Coach/Assessor) Signature

Name in capitals    **M. T. CLARKE**

**RYA DINGHY SAILING COACH ASSESSOR**

Please note it is also a requirement for instructors to hold a valid first aid certificate of a type approved by the RYA, and a Powerboat Level 2 certificate before progressing to the instructor training course.

## Training Course Completed
Venue      TIDAL/INLAND

Date

Course Organiser (RYA Coach/Assessor) Signature

Name in capitals

## Assessment/Moderation Completed
I confirm that the candidate has demonstrated competence as a Dinghy Instructor in a DINGHY/KEELBOAT/MULTIHULL (delete as appropriate) to the standards laid down by the RYA.

Venue      TIDAL/INLAND

Date

Approved by (RYA Coach/Assessor) signature

Name in capitals

# ADVANCED INSTRUCTOR ENDORSEMENT

## Assessment Completed

I confirm that the candidate has demonstrated competence as an Advanced Instructor to the standards laid down by the RYA.

Venue

Date

Approved by (RYA Coach/Assessor) Signature

Name in capitals

# KEELBOAT INSTRUCTOR ENDORSEMENT

## Assessment Completed

I confirm that the candidate has demonstrated competence as a Keelboat Instructor to the standards laid down by the RYA.

Venue

Date

Approved by (RYA Coach/Assessor) Signature

Name in capitals

# MULTIHULL INSTRUCTOR ENDORSEMENT

## Assessment Completed

I confirm that the candidate has demonstrated competence as a Multihull Instructor to the standards laid down by the RYA.

Venue

Date

Approved by (RYA Coach/Assessor) Signature

Name in capitals

# SENIOR INSTRUCTOR

## Recommendation

I confirm that the candidate is competent to plan, organise and run a course within the RYA National Sailing Scheme.

Signature (Principal)

Name in capitals

Recognised teaching establishment

Date

## Eligibility

Minimum age 18
Two years intermittent or one year full time instructing since qualifying as a Dinghy Instructor
RYA Safety Boat certificate or Level 4 certificate (pre-1996)
Valid first aid certificate of a type recognised by the Health and Safety Executive and covering the treatment of hypothermia.
Sailing ability to at least the standard of RYA Dinghy Instructor
Recommendation from Principal of an RYA recognised teaching establishment

## Training Course

I confirm that the candidate has successfully completed the course and has demonstrated competence in all the areas required.

Venue                                          TIDAL/INLAND

Date

Signature (Course Organiser) signature

Name in capitals

You should now send your completed logbook, first aid certificate, Safety Boat certificate and RYA membership number/certificate registration fee to your Regional Coach.

The candidate has completed all sections of the RYA Senior Instructor Award.

Signature (Regional Coach)

Name in capitals

## RYA CLUB RACING COACH/RACING INSTRUCTOR ENDORSEMENT

### Training Course Completed

Venue

Date

Approved by (RYA/RRTC) Signature

Name in capitals

First Aid Certificate

Type

Date of issue

Checked by (signature)

Name in capitals

Date

### National Coaching Foundation Courses

| Course title | Date | Tutor's signature |
|---|---|---|
| 1 | | |
| 2 | | |
| 3 | | |
| 4 | | |

# RYA RACING COACH

## First Aid Certificate

Type

Date of issue

Checked by (signature)

Name in capitals

## Coaching Experience

Details of dates, venues, class(es) coached and conditions must be entered in the Personal Log section on page 111.

I confirm that the candidate has completed the period of coaching experience.

Signature (RYA National Racing Coach)

Name in capitals

## National Coaching Foundation Key Courses

| Course title | Date | Tutor's signature |
|---|---|---|
| 1 | | |
| 2 | | |
| 3 | | |

## Training Course

I confirm that the candidate has completed all the requirements of the above courses.

Venue

Date

Signature (RYA National Racing Coach)

Name in capitals

## Award

The candidate has successfully completed all the requirements laid down by the RYA and is hereby appointed as an RYA Racing Coach for two years.

Signature (RYA National Racing Coach)

Name in capitals

Date                                   Revalidated on

## Specialist subjects (if appropriate)

# COACH/ASSESSOR

## Recommendation

I confirm that the candidate has the experience and technical competence to be trained as a Coach/Assessor with the RYA National Coaching Scheme.

Signature (Regional Coach)

Name in Capitals

## Training Course

I confirm that the candidate has successfully completed the course and has demonstrated competence in all the areas required.

Signature (Course Organiser)

Name in capitals

Details of dates, venue and conditions must be entered in the Personal Log on page 111.

## Task Experience

I confirm that the candidate has assisted with an RYA Instructor Course and Assessment.

Signature (RYA Coach/Assessor)

Name in capitals

The candidate has completed all the requirements and is hereby appointed as an RYA Coach/Assessor.

Signature (RYA National Coach)

Date

# EQUAL OPPORTUNITIES STATEMENT - RYA COACHING

As a National Governing Body of Sport, the RYA fully supports the principles of equal opportunities and is committed to ensure that all participants in its training and coaching schemes are treated fairly and on an equal basis, regardless of gender, age, racial origin, religious persuasion, sexual orientation or disability.

In formulating its schemes and assessment techniques, in operating its procedures and in producing its materials, the RYA seeks to avoid a format, language or approach which:

Is offensive to members of particular groups
Cannot be readily understood by some candidates
Does not have the same meaning for all candidates
Implies stereotyped or biased attitudes.

The RYA seeks to avoid inequality:

In the selection, recruitment and training of all those working for or on behalf of the Association

In the format and content of all syllabi, regulations, assessments and materials produced and/or distributed

Through the monitoring of its schemes operated at recognised teaching establishments.

By the relaxation of any regulations which serve to inhibit the performance of candidates with special needs in relation to candidates not so disadvantaged, provided that such action does not have a deleterious effect on the standard, quality and integrity of its schemes and assessments.

# APPEALS PROCEDURE

## *Assessment standards*

All RYA-qualified Instructors and Assessors are required to treat students and candidates with respect and fairness.

All assessments in the use of boats and their equipment have implications for the safety of participants. It is therefore essential that candidates are given a thorough and searching assessment. It would be dangerous to the candidate and anyone whom they subsequently teach if an Assessor erred on the side of leniency in awarding a certificate. There must never be any question of relaxing the standards required for an award.

## *Realistic aims*

In some cases, it becomes clear to the Assessor at an early stage in the assessment process that the candidate has been over-ambitious in their choice of award. In such instances the Assessor should discuss the situation with the candidate and agree revised achievable aims.

## *Grounds for appeal*

A candidate has grounds for appeal if he or she believes:
Either,
The they have not been given a reasonable opportunity to demonstrate their competence.
Or,
That they have been placed under undue or unfair pressure by the person carrying out the assessment.
Or,
That the Assessor has reached the wrong conclusion on the basis of the outcome of the candidate's performance in the assessment.

## *The procedure*

The candidate should first raise the concern with the Assessor to see if the matter can be amicably resolved. If it is inappropriate to consult the Assessor, or if there is no amicable solution, the candidate should appeal in writing to the RYA National Coach within 20 working days of the assessment. The letter of appeal should contain the following:

Full details of the assessment - when, where, involving whom etc
The nature of the appeal
Any supporting documentation relating to the assessment - outcome, action plans, reports etc.

On receipt of an appeal, an investigative process will commence. Following investigation, the candidate will be informed of the outcome, which will be one of the following:

The original decision confirmed

The assessment carried out again by the same or a different Assessor

The original decision overturned and the assessment judged to be adequate.

If the candidate is still unhappy about the decision, they may appeal against the outcome to the RYA's Training Divisional Committee.